I0462912

Become a Real Estate "Top Producer" in 12 Months

Alfredo Yaffe

Copyright © 2019

All Rights Reserved

ISBN:9781089568803

Dedication

This book is dedicated to my family.

To my wife, Gaby, who gets me out of bed bright and early every day and has stuck with me for the past 25 years through the ups and downs of my life.

To my son, Federico Yaffe, who joined me straight out of school and has been with me ever since. The two of us are always striving to grow.

To my other son, Fernando Yaffe, who's wild and eccentric charisma always has a way of brightening up my stressful days.

To Francine Yaffe and Flavia Yaffe, my amazing daughters who keep me young and on my feet! Lastly, my parents, Katiuska "Yiye" Yaffe and Leon Chelebi "Felipe" Yaffe, who made me the person I am today.

None of this would have been possible without the continued encouragement and motivation from all of you!

Last but not least, I would like to thank Richard H. Breslow Attorney at Law Esq. who has given me guidance and unconditional support over the years. Now, he is not only my Attorney, but also my dear friend.

Acknowledgment

Writing a book can be very time consuming. Putting together all the knowledge that I have attained over my years as a Real Estate Broker in South Florida is not an easy task. Thanking those who got me to where I am today is much easier. This book goes out to all Real Estate agents, past and present.

To the top producers and the emerging agents, those who have been with us throughout our journey, and those who have chosen different paths. All of them contributed to certain parts of this book, and without each and every one of them, this book would have never even been a thought.

CONTENTS

About the Author

Alfredo Yaffe is an accomplished real estate agent who is determined to help others do the same. He has always been a top producer, and he wants nothing less for other realtors. His real estate agency aims to follow the same ideology.

Yaffe has had an illustrious career in real estate since birth. The following is a list of events in his life in chronological order.

- 1961 – Born in Montevideo, Uruguay
- 1978 – Began working in the family business selling textiles, including managing the retail stores, administration, and company expansion.
- 1981 – Opened his first athletic wear store in Uruguay, eventually growing to over eight branches scattered across Uruguay
- 1990 – Started an athletic footwear wholesale operation, with sales to over a hundred retail stores in South America
- 1999 – President/CEO of ZA-ZA USA, Corp.

- 2004 - Worked for TIR International Realty along with Developers in Florida
- 2005 - Opened Yaffe International Realty a Real Estate with an aggressive commission split that allowed the company to amass hundreds of Agents
- 2014 - Opened "Bright Title Services" in a partnership with Richard Breslow Esq.
- 2015/2016 - Yaffe became a Participant of the Grievance Committee of the Residential Miami Association of Realtors.
- 2016 – Became a member of the Ethics Panel of the Professional Standards Committee at the Realtor Association of Miami Dade. Was appointed to serve on Ethics Hearings.
- 2016 – Appointed as Florida Realtors State Director.
- 2017 – Ombudsman Program Training.
- 2017 – Alfredo Yaffe, as Broker of Yaffe International Realty was invited to Washington D.C as one of the TOP 50 FLORIDA BROKERAGES.

- 2017/2018 - He has been successful in obtaining Real Estate designations, such as TRS – BPOR – CDPR – CLHMS

Yaffe International Realty

Alfredo Yaffe's company is based on its agents. They offer aggressive commission splits and free training. The training they give offers essential skills and covers topics such as: dealing with clients, ethics on how to treat customers, and how to attract clients. At Yaffe International Realty, we understand that when an agent begins a new chapter in his/her life, they need training and guidance, which is why Yaffe International Realty provides detailed training right at their office and virtually through the Yaffe University. One of the many benefits of working at Yaffe International Realty is that they have hands-on time with their marketer. Their director of marketing sits down and teaches their agents how to maximize exposure and how to create a database filled with leads.

When joining the company, new agents receive one-on-one guidance and an office manager sits with them throughout their first interactions and first deals with clients to teach them hands-on experience of learning real estate. All of the companys efforts are directed to help their agents close more deals, which has given them great results. In 2017, they managed to close more than 2,500 transactions, averaging 6.8 deals a day!

Preface

The book is a guide for those who seek to excel in their real estate careers. The chapters of this book will help you become the top real estate agent in just a matter of 12 months.

However, for this book to help you out as it intends to, you will have to religiously follow the path it shows you. I have shared all my life experiences as a real estate agent in this book, so whoever reads this book can get a clear guidance route towards success.

The first chapter of the book briefs you about what real estate is and whether it is for you or not. It tells you about the traits you are expected to have in your identity if you wish to become a top-notch real estate agent. Overall, the book will inform you of how to be successful, you will have to work tirelessly in the field of real estate; you must also be in contact with important people and should be aware of the constantly changing market.

This book will teach you the steps that you must

follow to become a top producer. You will also get to learn what you must and must not do when you receive the first call from a potential customer in great depth and detail. The book will guide you with respect to when you should arrange a meeting, what to do when the customer agrees to meet you at the specified time, and how to make the customers say 'yes,' among several other things.

The book will be with you from the starting point, guide you every step of the way, and help you meet your destiny as a successful real estate agent in just about a year.

How to Become a "Top Producer" in 12 month.

Chapter 1

Introduction

Every year thousands of people from all over the country try to enter the world of real estate with great hopes and ambitions. However, a majority of these people give up in the first few months. Out of those remaining, some of them manage to pull through while others keep on leaving one-by-one after failing miserably. Eventually, only a few hundred people make it and become successful real estate agents. These people are the ones who enter the real estate industry with full preparation, which gives them a great boost throughout their journey in this field.

If you are one of those people who aspire to become a successful real estate agent, then you need to be completely aware of the struggles and hardships of this industry. After getting through the hard part, there are great things to come. This book will help you understand each and everything you need to know before beginning your journey to becoming the top real estate producer.

Throughout my career as a real estate agent, I have seen many young enthusiastic people fail and succeed in this field. Being a real estate agent myself, I have been through all the good and bad experiences of the industry and came out on top. I have my own brokerage in Miami now, which is producing some pretty good numbers. I have over 14 years of experience in this field, which makes me perfectly qualified to write this book as a guide for the up and coming real estate agents of future generations.

This book is guaranteed to help you become the top

real estate agent in just twelve months. The only condition is that you have to follow the path that the book tells you to. I have incorporated all my life experiences as a real estate agent in this book, so whoever reads this book can get a clear guidance route towards success.

Is Real Estate for You?

Before we move ahead with discussing other important points, the first thing you need to do is ask yourself a question. The question is, is real estate really the field for you? To answer this question, you should be completely aware of what this industry is all about.

Real estate is basically a branch of sales. There is very little difference in selling a glass cleaner by going door-to-door and selling a big house to some wealthy customers. In the end, you just have to be a good salesman. However, a glass cleaner just costs a few dollars while a house can be somewhere in the region of hundreds of thousands and sometimes even millions of dollars. Therefore, you are more likely to sell a few glass cleaners by the end of the day but might have to wait a few months to sell the house. This means that being a real estate agent is exactly similar to being a normal salesman, but you need to have a bigger vision and be more patient. So, if you are interested in becoming a real estate agent and think you have the qualities of a good salesman, then the answer to the question above is definitely, yes. If you don't think that you can become a good seller, then it certainly means that this is not the field for you.

If you answered yes to the question mentioned

above, then keep on reading this book as it will guide you to become the best in the industry. You will learn about the mistakes that many people make in the beginning so you can avoid them and save your valuable time. Once you become successful, it may prove to be the best career choice and you will be set for life.

You Are Your Own Boss

As Realtors, we do not just sell properties, we sell our services!

One of the beauties of becoming a real estate agent is that even if you have to work for a Brokerage, you are an independent contractor, you are your own boss. There will be no restriction for you to clock in at 9 am and wait till 5pm to leave the office. You choose if, when, and where you set up meetings with your clients.

However, this doesn't mean that you wouldn't be required to work hard. In order to be successful, you will have to work tirelessly. You should always be in contact with important people and should be aware of the market constantly. Time management is the key in the real estate industry. No customer likes a real estate agent who doesn't take care of time and leaves them hanging at the last moment.

Being a boss means that you are on your own. That may be a blessing and also a curse if you aren't on the right path. Sure almost every real estate agent goes through the training to earn the license. However, the real learning happens in the market when you start exploring the areas and meeting clients.

Take a look at this example of a boxer:

A boxer receives training and tips from his coach. He puts in the hard work at the gym to prepare for the upcoming fight under the coach's supervision. However, after entering the ring on the fight day, the boxer is on his own. Every punch he throws or receives is entirely up to him, and the result of the fight depends on him entirely.

Similarly, the people that train you for real estate markets are your coaches, and once you enter the field, it is just like entering a boxing ring. The result of the fight is in your hands, and no one can change your destiny but yourself.

Be Prepared to Work with No Income

I have seen way too many give up too quickly when trying to make it in the real estate industry. Just like every other field, it is not that easy to get instant success. You should be financially prepared before beginning your journey as an independent real estate agent. Most of the realtors make no money at all in the first months of entering the industry. Make sure you and your family are financially prepared to face this hard time together. It can be a frustrating time, but pulling through it will certainly reward you with incredible success.

This book will also guide you on how to get through the initial tough days and how to ensure that you are on the right path. You will learn some incredible selling tips that will surely help you a lot in this field.

Who or What Are You Working For?

If you have decided to enter the incredibly challenging industry of real estate, then there must be a reason behind it. Some people I met enter this industry simply because they are bored with their 9 to 5 life with a low salary, while others opt for real estate so that they can provide a better living standard for their family. Hence, you need to answer this question as well before embarking upon your journey.

After answering this question, make your purpose your motivating factor. For example, if you are doing this to provide a better life for your children, then do it for them. Your children should be on your mind at all times to keep you motivated and prevent you from giving up too early.

Realtors might not be restricted to 9 to 5 working hours, but sometimes they have to work more hours than an average Joe. You might also be required to work over the weekends, which can be frustrating for many people. However, having your main goal in your head at all times can serve as a huge motivation factor during times like these, and will certainly keep you going.

Now that you have got a basic taste of what the field of real estate entails, it's time to look at the 15 principles that will certainly help you become a top producer real estate agent.

These are the 15 principles that you need to incorporate in your life in order to become a successful realtor:

1. Show Up

This field of real estate is incredibly demanding, which means you will have to make some serious changes in your day-to-day routine. It requires you to be healthy and active to take on the challenges of the field. This means you might be required to push your leisure activities aside to get as much time as possible for your upcoming challenge.

You might also be required to change your eating

habits. If you usually eat unhealthy food with poor nutrition, then replace it with healthy and highly nutritious food that can provide you with the necessary energy to stay active.

The real estate field demands you to present both mentally and physically at all times. In the first few months, you will most probably be working 24/7, which means you need to take care of your health to pull through this period. Having proper rest and putting the right amount of fuel in your body will certainly help you a lot in this field.

2. Follow Up

The real estate market runs on follow-ups. You should stay attentive at all times and be aware of all your clients. Make sure you develop long-lasting relationships with your clients. Make it good enough for them to feel comfortable with you so that they can openly tell you their desires. You should also be able to tell the hobbies of your clients.

Make sure to follow up relentlessly and professionally with every client. I usually tell my students to use *"fast and furious lead follow-up."* This approach means that you should be on your toes at all times. The faster you respond to any incoming inquiry, the better your chances are to close the deal. This is not just a theory, but a proven fact. If you want to be successful in this field, then you will have to be lightning fast in following-up.

3. Be Versatile

The real estate world is full of all kinds of people, which means you should be mentally prepared to deal with them. This also means that you will have to make some compromises with people that you don't exactly see eye to eye with. This demands incredible versatility, and you should possess it in order to succeed. You should be able to say 'yes' in a situation where you want to do the opposite just for the sake of making a sale.

For example, if a client calls in the middle of the night to go for a tour, then you should be ready to do so. It might be inconvenient and uncomfortable for you, but you should think about the possible sale, your commission, and your reputation in the market.

4. Be Creative in Your Solutions

One thing I have learned in this career is that being rigidity costs you money. You should be accommodating and creative when it comes to solving your problems.

The experiences that you are going to have as a realtor will change you as a person. Making positive changes with the right approach will give you the upper hand with future deals. Master the art of the deal and don't be afraid to get creative.

5. Recognize That Repetitious Boredom Pays Off

If you believe that by becoming a realtor you will get out of the repetitious and monotonous routine of 9 to 5, then you are wrong. Even the realtors have to deal with repetitious tasks most of the time. You have to call a pre-determined amount of customers each and every day. Remember, perseverance is the key to success. Throughout the day, repeat the same thing all over again until you grab someone's interest. However, the reward, in the end, will certainly be more fruitful than the rewards you get from an average job.

6. Never Practice "Self-Agency"

To become a realtor, you have to be selfless. I have seen many people who get full of themselves after being successful for a short period, which makes them confident in themselves that the clients would contact them instead of having to follow-up. This approach halts your growth and leaves you in the same position for a long period.

Just like normal sales, service matters a lot in the real estate market. You should be able to make your clients feel special in order to develop a good reputation in the market. It doesn't matter how impressive your portfolio becomes; you should always be able to serve your clients and follow them around. Just remember one rule in this industry, the more people you help, the wealthier you will become.

7. Be the Best at What Matters

So you have just become a realtor and success seems to be at your feet. Sadly, things aren't that simple in real life. Just like every other industry, there is a lot of competition in the real estate market. To stand out in this competition, you need to make sure that you are the best at everything that can help you become successful.

The things that a realtor should be great at are follow-ups, presentations, and pre-qualifying, persuasive skills, negotiating, and closing. All you have to do is master these skills, and the rest of the things will automatically fall into place.

8. Never Compromise by Settling for Mediocrity

As I have mentioned earlier, you should always give your best at everything when working as a realtor. There should be no room for compromises in any department. If you have an assistant or a team working for you, then you should always instruct them to strive to ensure the best service.

Every shortcoming can deliver a considerable dent on your reputation in the market. Imagine visiting a coffee shop to sip some refreshing hot beverage, but it turns out that the staff at that coffee shop treats you poorly. As a result, you will ensure that next time you avoid that coffee shop and go to its competitor instead. This is exactly how your performance affects your clients in the real estate market.

9. Systemize and Automate Before You Hire People

So you have finally made it as a successful realtor. But now your clientele has reached a remarkable number and it is getting difficult for you to manage all of them at once. What do you do then? Well, you hire some workforce. Before you do that, you need to develop a proper system and consider automation instead. If you need an extra hand, then go for hiring a person or a group of people.

After hiring some people, you need to teach them your methods and etiquettes. It is your business, which means you are in charge of how things run around here. After getting your employees in the mix, make sure you oversee their work unless it reaches a satisfactory level.

10. Adapt to Changes

Just like every other industry in the world, real estate is also constantly changing. Modifications are constantly on the high and to stay on course with the market, you should definitely adapt to these changes.

For example, a few years ago, the only way people were able to look for real estate was through newspapers and phonebooks that provided them the numbers of the agencies. However, since the advent of the internet, things have changed drastically. More and more people are now searching for real estate online. Therefore, having an online presence is a must in today's world. You should at least have a website and multiple social media accounts so that people can find you easily.

11. ABC – Always Be Closing

Closing is the goal, whether it's the sale, contract, or just an appointment in the real estate industry. You should always be striving for closing from your end and ensuring that the client has received more than satisfactory service. The fact that someone has given you their valuable time shows that they are interested. You need to make sure that you follow up with your clients to get their final decision so you can close the deal.

12. Follow One Path Until Successful

Adopt a system then stick to it until you get some success. Yes, change is good and you should definitely opt for a change but only when the time is right. Sticking to the right path will make you the master of that particular strategy, which means that if you are unable to adapt to a change in the future, then you can always retreat to your system in which you are most comfortable.

13. Take Some Risks

In the real estate industry, there is no such thing as 'try.' It's either do or don't do. This means that you will be required to take some risks if you want to move forward.

Holding back will surely keep you in a safe place, but eventually, you will have to find a way to rise above your competition, and this involves risk-taking.

In the end, real estate is a business, and you simply cannot expand your business without taking some risks.

14. Answer the Phone

As a realtor, a phone is the ultimate magic stick that is going to make you earn money. You should always be in the reach for your customers no matter what. Your clients should be your ultimate priority, as they are your main source of income. Ignoring someone constantly over the phone is considered to be rude, and this behavior certainly drives the clients away. Even if by chance you miss a call from a client, make sure to call them back or leave a message that you will call them later when free. This act shows the clients that you care about them, and they will happily wait for you.

15. Don't be a Secret Agent

Many people I have met tend to hide their profession in social conversations. I usually encourage my agents to reveal their profession to strangers and use it as a topic of conversation. You will be surprised to see how many deals you will be able to close while just hanging out with a group of people at a bar.

In this chapter, we learned the fifteen principles which you should engrave in your mind and follow to flourish in your career. In the next chapter, we will discuss how to become a top producer.

Chapter 2

Top Producer

"In the real estate business, you learn more about community issues; you learn more about life, you learn more about the impact of the government, probably more than any other profession that I know of."

- ***Johnny Isakon***

A real estate agent is a pretty distinctive career path when compared to your everyday job. It can either be the best career choice, while others might struggle a lot. It requires hard work, determination, and most importantly, patience.

People enter the world of real estate for many reasons. Some do it because they are struggling to make a decent living in their current career path, some do it because they want to support their family, others want to achieve their dreams that they couldn't while working their previous jobs. Whatever the reasons that compelled you to join this challenging profession, I urge you to keep that in the back of your mind the entire time you are working in this field. That's because it is an incredibly demanding profession that will often push you to your limits, and that is why many people burn out and quit. You should use that reason as motivation to carry yourself through some of the tough spots of becoming the top real estate agent of your territory.

The road to becoming a top producer is full of hurdles, and you will have to go through several sleepless nights to achieve your ultimate objective. It won't be like your ordinary job where no matter how bad your day goes, you will get off at 5 pm every day and even get to enjoy your weekends off. You will have to work beyond 5 pm and even sometimes on the weekends. However, if my decades of experience has taught me one thing about this field it is that if you keep reminding yourself the reason why you are doing this, all these exhausting long hours will go by in a jiffy.

As a top producer, you will have to serve as a bridge that connects the buyers and the sellers. If anything goes wrong with the deal, both parties will vent their frustrations on you. These moments will be one of the biggest challenges of your career, and if you are a new agent, you might get puzzled in such situations. Instead of panicking, you should focus on closing the deal at all costs, even if it means that you make little to no money on the deal. That's because your reputation in the market matters a lot. Disgruntled and dissatisfied clients have a negative impact on your portfolio, and you should never let that happen.

The real challenges begin when you go out in the field on your own. Working at a firm as a real estate agent might be the easiest part of this career. As an employee, you are still at a learning stage, and you have a manager who trains you. Therefore, firms tolerate mistakes made by young real estate agents who are new to the business. The firm nurtures them before they go out on their own.

You might have someone looking out for you when you are working and developing your skills at the firm, but once you are out there in the field, you are your own boss. When you are visiting properties with customers, you are the boss, and you control how the deal goes. Clients do not care if you are new or experienced; they want the best service and someone they can rely on to make that happen. This is where you will have to test your training and the skills that your firm gave you.

A boxer's analogy fits perfectly in this scenario. Imagine you are a boxer and there's a big fight coming up in a couple of months. What would you do? Of course, you would hire a trainer or coach who would prepare you for the fight. You will learn how to defend yourself while also mastering different combinations of punches such as hooks, jabs, uppercuts, etc. The coach will make sure that you are perfectly trained for the big day. However, on the day of the fight, from the moment you enter the ring, you will be on your own. Everything you learned from the coach will come in handy on that day, but it will be totally up to you how you utilize your skillset in the best possible way. You may also have to improvise a lot of techniques on the spot because you are unaware of what your opponent has in store. It will be entirely up to you how you win the match.

To become a top producer, you need to gain some training and experience by joining a brokerage firm. Going out there on your own without any guidelines and mentorship is a terrible idea, and it would be similar to a boxer entering the ring without any training. You are bound to lose this way.

How do you figure out which firm's the best for you? As an experienced brokerage owner and a real estate agent myself, I have developed a checklist for you that can help in determining whether the firm you want to join is good enough or not.

The brokerage you are about to join should fulfill the following qualities:

- **Training:** Not all real estate companies offer training to their new employees. Most of the brokerages will put you straight to the test because for them the training you obtained while you were getting your license (depends on the state you live in) is enough. Therefore, you need to look for a company that provides you training and develops your skillset before sending you out in the field to deal with clients.
- **Support:** You also need to look for companies that offer you support in finding good deals and help you out while you are on the field. The manager of the brokerage should also act as a mentor to the young agents and support them if they fail early in their practice. A kid does not learn to ride a bike in one day. Therefore, you cannot nail it the first time by landing a deal. A good support team behind you will help you in sharpening your selling skills to get you ready for all kinds of challenges when you go out on your own.
- **Programs/Software:** Another thing that should be on your checklist before you join a brokerage firm is the programs or software the company uses. You will be surprised to find out that many real estate companies still work in the old school way, manually. We are living in a digital age where the internet has brought everything within our reach. There are tons of real estate programs and software available in the market that agents are utilizing to make their lives easier. Agents are also active on the internet through popular real estate websites where clients are looking for

agents to guide them to the property of their desire.

- **Commission Split:** Commission split is one of the most important factors that you need to consider before nodding to join a firm. Independent agents pocket full commission, but that's because they have to find their own clients. Since you will be working for a company, they will help you find clients and therefore, you will have to share your commission with the firm. So, look for the company that offers a good and fair commission split.

- **Office Location:** When you look for a regular job, you prefer that the workplace is as close to your home as possible. In the world of real estate; however, you should look for a company that is located in the best area of town. That's because you are going to get better deals in an exotic area and probably pocket more commission as well.

The checklist mentioned-above will narrow down the list of suitable real estate firms for you, and you can pick the best out of the available options in your area.

I regularly meet a lot of young real estate agents aspiring to become top producers. They often ask me this question, "Which company should we join to develop ourselves as top producers?" After telling them to create the checklist, I advise them to visit at least four companies before settling for the one.

The reason I tell everyone to consider at least four companies is to consider other options. It is essential because if you still feel uncomfortable after joining a firm, you can switch to a place that you are familiar with.

The basic process for any realtor is the numbers game, where they should remember the following steps:

1. Goals

Goals are the most important thing that you need to consider before you set out on your path of becoming a top producer. On average, new, full-time agent earn an average of $35,000 annually. Therefore, you need to set your goals for the first three years. If you want to become a Top Producer, you need to know exactly where you are going, what you are going to achieve both in the short and long run and aim for it. It's very important to aim high to achieve higher results.

Let's assume that you set a goal of earning $100,000 in your first year (remember to set your goals high, and they will happen). If by average a closing can give you 3% of the selling price, then let's do the math. If the average property price in your market is $300,000, then it means you will earn $9,000 in commission (let your brokerage take whatever it takes). Let's assume you have a commission split of 80/20 with the brokerage, so out of the $9,000 the brokerage will take $1,800 and you will get $7,200.

$100,000 / $7,200 = 14

This calculation shows that you only need 14 transactions annually to reach your goal.

You can also achieve your goal through rentals, but it will take a lot more transactions to achieve the same goal. Let's say you do 40 rental transactions in a year. The average rent in your area is $1,800, and by average you get half of the first month's rent. As per this calculation, you may earn approximately $900 per transaction (minus your commission split with the brokerage). Reducing 20% from

$900 leaves you with $720.

$720 x 40 transactions = $28,800.

Therefore, it is better to focus on the 14 sale/purchase transactions that you need to close in the year. How can you do it? Focus on prospecting and marketing/advertising. Note that I said FOCUS on prospecting and marketing/advertising. You are going to realize when you manage your time for every task that you will need to focus on it to maximize your efforts to achieve your goal.

2. Knowledge of Your Farm Area

Your farm area is one where you are an expert. It can be your neighborhood or any other area where you feel comfortable working. In this particular area, you need to know where are all the banks, schools (elementary, middle and high school), grocery stores, and of course, the median price of properties in the area. You can check the prices on your MLS (Multiple Listing Service). The more you know, the better. Be THE SPECIALIST in your AREA as this is the place where you should be directing your marketing/advertising efforts.

3. Knowledge of Contracts

Of course, I assume you have some knowledge about the contracts and addenda because brokerages normally give you some training on that matter.

Important Notice: Always read all Sale/Purchase contracts and addenda at least once a year. If you do not understand any part, ask your broker or manager about it. Remember that if a customer asks you something about the contract/offer that you want him/her to sign, then you should be able to respond and explain to them the meaning of that as well. Customers trust you. They will only understand what you tell them to sign on. Many people don't bother reading the terms listed in a contract because it is a tedious job. Therefore, you must explain it to them if they fail to understand any part of the contract.

4. Time Management

We all get the same 24 hours in a day. Why is it that some people achieve so much more in their time compared to others?

The answer is simple.

Sucessful people focus on time management.

Time management is the process of organizing and planning how much time you spend on specific activities.

To become a top producer, you need to have top-notch time management skills.

A typical realtor's morning routine should be somewhat like the following:

- 9 am to 10 am, making calls to all prospects.
- 10 am to 11 am, focus on marketing/advertising.
- 11 am to 1 pm, hold meetings with the clients.

The routine mentioned above is just an example that I came up with. You can schedule it however you like.

5. Prospecting

As a real estate agent, the first thing you need to do is have as many customers as possible. That's because it increases the probability of success. Prospecting helps real estate agents in ensuring a steady stream of client listings.

Prospecting is a really important step in the sales process. It involves looking for potential clients and then persuading them to convert them into actual clients. Successful agents dedicate some of their valuable time each week specifically for prospecting. One of the major benefits of prospecting is that it helps you in building relationships with clients. For example, if you manage to sell a property for a client successfully, they may also help you in future prospecting. Furthermore, that client may also help you in attracting other potential clients through referrals.

The following are some of the tips that you can use for prospecting:

- Keep in touch with the clients that you have worked with in the past for referrals.
- Call clients who recently had a failed deal with other agents. Explain to them why you are better than the previous agent they worked with.
- Contact ads that show, "For sale by Owner." However, you might need to persuade them why they need an agent for getting a good price by selling their property.
- Hold free real estate seminars. Choose topics that will attract your potential clients to your services such as, "Tips for selling your home for a good price."

6. Leads

In the beginning, creating new leads for your business is the only important task on your tab. However, after a while, you have a huge pipeline that keeps giving out leads of its own, through referrals or otherwise.

Then comes the conversion stage when you have to convert these leads into your actual customers. It might seem like a difficult task, but if you have the right knowledge regarding your field and the scripts, then you will have no problem at all.

Here's an example of a conversation between a real estate agent and a customer (of a rental listing) from a marketplace:

Customer: is this available?

(Remember that they just clicked on your ad and automatically appeared in your messenger, "is this available?")

Agent: Yes

With this response, this conversation is over 90% of the times at this point. Here, the agent didn't do their job properly. They are not looking to create a conversation that will lead to a meeting with this person in order to know their Real Estate needs.

The conversation should be like the following:

Customer: Is this available?

Agent: Yes, when do you need to move?

At this point, the agent is to get the customer's attention to their listing. On average, about 70% of the customers respond to this question. Once that customer responds, we will continue. Remember that our goal is for this customer to come to our office and meet them. Let's see how this conversation progresses.

Customer: I need to move in one month.

Agent: Great, the association on this condo unit takes approximately three weeks for approval on new tenants. Can you come to our (Office City) office tomorrow at 11 am so we can visit this property and other similar ones so we have more than one place to evaluate and you can get the one that you prefer?

Customer: No, I cannot visit your office till 5 PM as I get off from work by that time. Can I come over by 6 PM?

Agent: Of course, let me give you my office address.

Customer: Great

Agent: Please provide your contact number for confirming tomorrow's appointment.

(Please note that if the customer does not provide their contact number, the meeting stays unconfirmed.)

Customer: You can contact me on: xxx-xxx-xxxx

Agent: Thanks!

Important note: After that, the agent must send a text message to the prospect with something like the following:

Hi, this is "Agent's Name." I have scheduled a showing for the property you are interested in tomorrow XYZ Day at 6 PM. Please reply to this message with a 'Yes,' if your appointment is confirmed. To reschedule your appointment, reply with, 'No.'

If a customer replies with a Yes, then they will definitely visit you. Contact customer one hour before the meeting to confirm it if you don't receive any answer from the client. If the customer replies with 'No,' send them other possible dates and timings for their appointment to choose from.

Keep in mind that the process of creating and retaining leads is an endless cycle. You cannot stop looking because you have found a few good ones. You should never slow down your marketing efforts because they have already brought in leads. I have seen many successful realtors fail miserably, because they gave up on their efforts to pursue more leads. If you cannot keep up with marketing/advertising, then hire help, but never put a stop to your efforts.

Always remember that real estate is a numbers game. You have to get a certain number of leads to get the customers you need to make maximum profits. After some time, you will start seeing a percentage of leads that end up becoming your clients. For example, out of 10 leads, you may be converting 5 of them into your customers. Although it is a very good conversion rate, you should keep working on improving it.

So, the question that might arise in your mind is, "how do I convert my leads into clients?"

The answer is simple, follow the scripts. There are many generic scripts that real estate agents use to convert their leads into clients, and they seem to work most of the time. Of course, you don't need to memorize a script word by word. You can add or remove anything you feel necessary. There is no such thing as the 'perfect script.' You can use anything that works for you.

A top producer should never follow a single strategy. Instead, they should keep on trying different methods to market their services. For example, I have seen many people clinging on to just postcards even if it is not working for them. What they don't seem to realize is that other agents have already sent postcards to their leads and have converted them into their customers.

The main idea here is to learn from your mistakes. If the postcard technique doesn't seem to be working for you, then you should move on to do something different that does work. This reminds me of a wonderful story about an art teacher's lesson to his students.

An art teacher separated the students in his class into two groups. He gave them a task to design decorative vases for the entire day. One group was given the task to focus on quality rather than quantity. The teacher told them that they would be judged upon the quality of the work at the end of the day.

He told the second group that they would be judged by the number of vases they decorate throughout the day. So the group of students started working on their projects.

The first group picked up only one vase and decided to work on it for the whole day since they only had to focus on quality. They used the best colors and designs they could possibly come up with to decorate their vase.

The second group started working on as many vases as they could. They started with poor designs that were done in a hurry as they had their focus on doing as much as they can.

By the end of the day, the teacher took a look at the finished projects of his students. The first group presented their only vase, which was brilliant from their perspective. However, the teacher pointed out a few mistakes in the finished product. The second group presented a total of 100 vases. The first few ones were terrible, but as they had moved further and created more, the 20th or so vases got better and so on. The last vase that they finished was not only their best work, but it was also a lot better than the one made by the first group. The second group won the competition.

The moral of the story is that getting better at anything requires time and testing. It is a gradual process. You cannot nail something in the first attempt. Therefore, if you are unable to convert leads into clients, then keep on trying different methods. You will surely succeed in the end.

"You will never know if you can achieve something unless you try. You lose very little by trying and win the most by succeeding."

7. Schedule Appointments

A great real estate agent should be familiar with the wants and needs of their clients. Prospecting will give you an idea about the kinds of properties that could attract your potential clients. Therefore, you should lure them by sending pictures and videos of available properties. Similarly, you should ask for images and videos of the property from sellers.

Once you get approval from the interested party, the next thing you need to do is schedule an appointment with potential clients.

Scheduling appointments beforehand is really important in the real estate business; neither you nor your clients would be free enough to be available on call. Be punctual in meeting your clients on the decided time as it matters a lot.

8. Showings

Showing or touring of the properties with the clients is where you are going to learn the most. It is right there where you will find out about the likes and dislikes of your clients. You can use this information to persuade them to buy/rent any property. For example, if you show a client a house with a big backyard, and they immediately say, "It's perfect because I have two dogs." You might not be aware of this particular fact that your client had pets. Therefore, you can use this information to persuade your next client. If you show a similar house to a different client, you can ask, "Do you have pets, because this house has a big backyard that would be perfect for them."

One rule you have to keep in mind during showings is that you must always mention positive things about the property. If there's a wall painting that you do not like, then you don't need to mention it. You may never know, your client may like it. However, it doesn't mean that you should hide flaws about the property from your clients as it would be counted as cheating. If there's something you need to disclose, go ahead and disclose it. For example, if there is rough flooring in one area of the house, then you should inform the client about it and advise them to get it inspected by a professional to make sure it's not severely damaged or anything.

I always advise my clients to have a full inspection of the property by professionals to determine if it is satisfactory for them.

9. Listings

Listings are really important for realtors. There is a famous saying that, "If you list, you last." Once you are able to acquire listings of the properties, you can do the following things:

- You won't have to deal with the stress of building your listing inventory
- You are going to make a whole lot of money in less time as all real estate agents would be working to find a buyer for you

10. Contracts

As a realtor, you should be familiar with all sorts of contracts that you are going to deal with. Usually, real estate agents work alongside lawyers because some of the contracts they have to deal with are legally binding. However, it is important for you to familiarize themselves with these contracts as well.

Understanding the contracts can help you lead clients to a smoother transaction and solidify your reputation as a bona fide realtor in your area.

Listed below are some types of contracts that you may have to deal with as a realtor:

- **Residential Sale/Purchase Contract:** It is required when the client finally decides to make a purchase. This contract contains all the essential details of the purchase. It is also the most common type of real estate agreement.
- **Exclusive Brokerage Contracts:** Although rarely used, the exclusive contracts are required in the case where the buyer and the seller have different agents. Signing these contracts gives exclusive rights to agents on both sides of the parties to the contract.

- **Financing Addendum:** This type of contract is required when the buyer needs to complete a financing addendum first before making the purchase.

11. Closing

After all negotiation is done, all paperwork is handled with the parties involved, including brokerage, mortgage, Title Company, etc. the only thing left is the closing. Closing refers to the transferring of the property from one owner to another. Closing is a big deal for us realtors as it often takes a lot of time to get to this point. We have to go through a lot of stages to reach here, such as negotiations, renegotiations, inspections, fulfilling mortgages and title requests, etc. Closing is considered as a victory for realtors as it is at this point that the commissions for the brokerage are finally disbursed.

12. CRM

Once you have closed a transaction, you must place it on your CRM and create drip emails according to the transaction.

Remember that you NEED to do your follow up and the CRM will help you in sending drip Emails, scheduling meetings, etc. Check if your real estate company has a CRM system. If not, you can have access to many of those at a very low cost in the market.

13. $$$$

As realtors, we only make money when the deal is finally closed. It might seem like an easy process for the clients, but only we know what we have to go through to reach this stage.

Customers are unaware of the immense amount of work that real estate agents have to do to earn their payout. If there is anything wrong with the property, it automatically becomes our problem to solve. For example, if there is an electrical issue at the property, we will have to fix it. Similarly, if there is any other kind of problem with the property, the client will ring us to get it fixed. We have to act like a "fuse" between the clients and all problems that they spot on the property, and we have to do it just so the client is satisfied enough to close the deal finally.

14. Hire Help

Before hiring the right person, you need to write down all the duties that you expect this person to do and how they will be doing the job.

You need to have a system in place. Teach about the system and how things work to your new assistant and make sure that they understand what you are expecting of them. The assistant must have work-related goals/targets that are aligned with yours.

Let's say you want your assistant to work on marketing/advertising and create presentations for listings. The assistant's first target is to schedule 3 listing presentation meetings per week.

You need to tell the assistant which advertising should be used and where it should be placed. Teach them the script that they need to use when talking with potential seller's, with FSBO, etc.

Be clear with what your expectations are, and the duties your assistant needs to fulfill.

It is not easy to find a great assistant. If they are

failing to achieve all their targets, then you need to look for someone else.

You may also hire an assistant merely for just the paperwork (administrative) and/or listing agent or a buyers agent. My first advice is to hire an administrative assistant who is going to take care of all the paperwork and make your life a lot easier. This way you can only focus on prospecting, marketing/advertising, and working with leads.

After hiring an administrative assistant, you can hire a seller's or buyer's assistant.

Your help must serve as a leverage in your team's productivity. That's why the assistant must be accountable and should be aware of their duties and goals to make it happen.

Responsibilities of a Seller's Agent

- Arrange and make listing presentations.
- Prospecting
- Work with Seller's leads
- Sign listing contracts,
- Place the listings on the MLS
- Place signs on the property
- Do Open Houses
- Marketing for the property (Social Media, postcards to neighbors.
- Send a report every Friday to sellers regarding the property (including updates on the market)

Responsibilities of a Buyer's Agent

- Make advertising looking for buyers
- Prospecting

- Work with Buyer's leads.
- Arrange meetings with potential buyers and search properties
- Make the buyer to be a prequel (if they need it)
- Show Properties
- Make offers on properties on behalf of buyers
- Negotiate the offers according to the needs of customers.
- Execute contracts
- Send executed contracts to Title Company and Loan Officer (if needed).
- Deal on all the items and contingencies till the closing date.
- Close the Deal!

15. Follow-Up

After you have closed the deal with a customer, you need to keep in touch with them for follow-up. You should aim to make all your clients your customers for life. That's because they can help you in earning other potential clients through referrals. Following-up with the client will give them the impression that you care about them, and they will happily refer you to their friends and family.

16. Referrals

One of the things you need to do after satisfying a client by closing a deal with them is to ask them for referrals. A happy client would certainly refer you to their social circles, which means you will be able to acquire more clients.

How to Become a "Top Producer" in 12 month.

To become a top producer, you need to go through grueling days of sleepless nights and endless working hours. However, you cannot learn all these skills on your own, so the best way to start is by joining a real estate brokerage. A real estate brokerage will help you in the real estate process and teach you how to become a top producer.

Chapter 3

Training

"To be successful in real estate, you must always and consistently put your client's best interests first. When you do, your personal needs will be realized beyond your greatest expectations."

- *Anthony Hitt*

Ganbaru (頑張る lit., stand firm), romanised as 'Gambaru,' is a ubiquitous Japanese word which roughly means to slog on tenaciously through tough times. The word Ganbaru is often translated to mean "doing one's best," but in practice, it means doing more than one's best.

That's what you have to do in your real estate career; do your best to become the best! You can't just walk into any line of work and instantly ace it. You need to get the necessary training, just like every other person on the planet. The same story goes when we talk about the real estate industry. I would suggest you look for a real estate brokerage that has some training programs as well before shoving you straight into the field.

Becoming a top producer real estate agent is a long and gruelling process for some people. Not everyone is gifted with flawless communication skills and fast learning abilities. However, if you work hard with immense determination, then you can certainly make it big in this industry. The main thing is that you need to go through a training regime to become a top producer first.

I have prepared a list of major steps that I often suggest to new agents, who are still going through a learning process, at my brokerage. The following are the steps that you should follow if you desire to become a top producer in the real estate industry:

Step 1: Find Out If You Possess the Skills

If your aspiration to become a real estate agent came from watching movies or TV shows, then you are in for a big surprise. Films and TV shows portray real estate agents as the smartest people on earth with dashing looks and expensive convertible cars. Sure, presentation matters a lot in a job where you meet other people, but it is not the most important thing. You should look out for the necessary skills that will help you excel in this field. Listed below are some of the skills that you should incorporate in your real estate career if you don't already have them:

1. You Don't Have To Be "People's Person."

Social skills are incredibly important in the field of real estate as your main job is to meet people and show them around the properties. However, the people that you are going to meet are embarking on one of the most important and expensive journeys of their lives. They would care more about you being trustworthy rather than just being an excellent communicator. That's because what you say is often more important than how you say it. Therefore, you need to be straight forward but still have the capacity to convince people.

2. Be Self-Motivated

As a real estate agent, you don't work for anyone but yourself. Sure you can be a part of a brokerage, but the broker who is sponsoring you isn't exactly your boss. They can't force you to come to the office since they aren't paying you any salary. Therefore, all of your success as a real estate agent lies solely on your own shoulders. If you work hard enough, you can progress positively in this field and may even develop a bigger portfolio to separate yourself from the brokerage and work completely on your own.

3. Professional Background Helps But Isn't Necessary

Many people believe that you need to have some professional experience in order to become a top producer in the real estate industry. Prior experience is certainly quite helpful, but it is not needed. Some of the most successful people in the world of real estate didn't have any professional background before they decided on becoming a real estate agent.

4. Possess Marketing and Advertising Skills

Another set of skills that you need to master are marketing and advertising. As a real estate agent, it should be your prime target to attract as many clients as possible to avail your services. The more clients you deal with, the higher your chances are to close a deal.

Marketing and advertising have become quite easier and less expensive, thanks to the internet. You can utilize social media, SEO, and many other online marketing methods to target your potential customers. Also, you have to be active on famous real estate websites such as Realtor, Zillow, and many others. Having your own website is a huge plus.

5. Have Top-Notch Negotiation Skills

Negotiation skills are one of the most important things that you need to have to become a top producer in the real estate world. You should be able to communicate over phone, email, text, and in person with the same intensity and efficiency. You should also be able to interact with customers professionally and have facts and figures and comparisons of the properties on the tip of your tongue.

6. Delicate Customer Service Skills

As a real estate agent, your primary function at the end of the day is to provide your customers with services regarding the selling, purchasing, or renting of property at their desired prices. However, it isn't as easy and straightforward as it seems. There will be a lot of concerns and problems that your clients will go through before making a decision. During this phase, you need to develop your customer service skills. You should eliminate all their worries and concerns by giving them certain assurances and handling tasks for them. In this way, you will earn their trust, and they will most likely consider your services the next time as well. People who possess great customer skills go a long way in the real estate business.

7. Be Ready for "No Days Off"

If you are not comfortable working late or weekends, then you should look elsewhere. Many people looking for real estate services will most likely contact you after 6 PM or over the weekend. Therefore, you need to be prepared for working some extra hours if you want to be successful in this line of work.

8. Be Prepared to Work Without Any Income

When it comes to working as a real estate agent, there are no assurances on how much money you are going to make, especially if you are new to this field. You might not even make a dime in the first few months. Therefore, before joining this immensely challenging industry, you must have enough savings that will last you at least 3 to 6 months when you commence your business.

Step 2: Register for a Pre-Licensing Course

The next step that you need to take, in order to become a real estate agent, is to sign up for a real estate pre-licensing course. This course is available in all states of the country and considered necessary before you can take the exam. The registration cost for the course is somewhere between $99 and $649. It may even be higher depending on the state you are residing in and also the school you choose to attend. This pre-licensing course is really helpful, and it strengthens your basics about the industry.

Step 3: Take the Licensing Exam

After you have successfully completed the pre-licensing course and training, you need to take the exam. I recommend that you apply for the exam immediately after completing the course since the concepts you have learned in classes will be fresh in your mind. That's because the paperwork in the application process can take some time. Therefore, the sooner you apply for the exam, you will have a shorter waiting time.

The test can be a bit difficult if you aren't prepared for it. The format of the exam varies from state to state.

Typically, it's a multiple-choice questionnaire that usually takes somewhere between 1.5 and 3 hours to complete. The exam includes all national and state laws and principles. The passing ratio is 70 to 75 percent.

Passing this test is important as it will grant you the license to work as a real estate agent. Many people tend to fail the test in their first attempt due to poor preparation. Since you are going to invest your time and money in pre-licensing courses, you need to make sure to pass this in your first try to avoid frustration.

Step 4: Join a Brokerage

After you successfully pass your exams with flying colors, you need to look for a suitable brokerage and join it. This is a major step that almost every real estate agent has to go through before they stand on their own two feet and start working for themselves. You need a real estate broker to sponsor you because you need to understand the market before doing head-first into the real estate industry.

The question that might arise in your mind at this point is: who's a real estate broker, and why do I need to be sponsored by them? A sponsor is required for you to get the license. A real estate broker is someone who has earned extensive experience in the industry and who also holds a brokerage license. This license grants them the authority to run their own real estate business and hires agents to work for them. In a typical brokerage, agents work in the field while the broker oversees transactions and takes some liability away from them.

There are tons of choices to make when it comes to brokerages. You have national franchises and small boutique brokerages. Each of them has their own commission splits and desk fees. Of course, considering these factors is important as it determines how much money you make as a real estate agent.

Finding a good brokerage is pretty easy these days. You can either go for an old fashioned approach by asking around fellow agents or go straight to the internet. Since most of the brokerages have some online presence nowadays, it will only take a few minutes for you to find the right one in your area.

Working for a brokerage is essential because it is a great way to learn and develop your skills. Consider the broker, who's sponsoring you, as your mentor and learn from them the craft of closing a deal. After you have acquired enough experience, you can walk out of the brokerage and start working independently.

Step 5: Apply for Real Estate License

After you have found the broker who is willing to sponsor you, the next step you need to take is to apply for a real estate license. One of the application requirements are the transcripts of the pre-licensing course. Another requirement is the ID number of the broker who is sponsoring you along with your Social Security Number, and you own state ID (e.g., a driver's license).

The application fees vary from state to state. Some states may also ask you to submit a background check and there may be some additional fees for these procedures.

Step 6: Join the National Association of Realtors (NAR)

After receiving your license, the next step you should do is join the National Association of Realtors (NAR). This is an optional step that you can skip if you like, but I recommend you to do it because of the benefits.

You might have heard the word "realtor" being used by many real estate agents to refer to themselves. However, not every real estate agent can call themselves a realtor as this term is exclusive for the members of the NAR members only. You can acquire the privilege of calling yourself as a realtor by joining NAR.

The fees for joining NAR is roughly between $200 and $500 per year.

Some of the major benefits of joining NAR are:

- You will have an automatic list sharing agreements with all the other members of your local realtor's association.
- If one member lists a house for sale, all the other members are allowed to show the property to potential buyers and collect a commission on the sale if it gets sold.
- NAR also has a code of ethics that all the realtors are bound to follow. This ensures everything goes smoothly, without any problems.

It is possible to work as real estate agents without acquiring membership of NAR. However, it would be a huge mistake not to join it. The membership is not expensive, and its benefits outweigh its cost.

All of these steps mentioned here are important for you to follow in the same order if you are aspiring to become a top producer.

The next thing you need to incorporate in your

training is to learn about the different types of contracts. As a real estate agent, you will have to deal with a lot of contracts daily. Therefore, you need to be fully trained for the occasion by learning what kinds of contracts are involved in the industry and how to sign and oblige them.

For example, here in South Florida, we commonly have to deal with contracts such as the contract to lease, residential lease for a condo, residential leases for a single home, etc.

In order to get familiar with the contracts, you have to ask for a copy of contracts, addendum, and special clauses from the brokerage where you are working. If you face any confusion in the contract or a clause, then you can ask any broker/manager to explain it to you.

Here are some of the contracts that you need to learn about before heading out on your own to deal with the customers:

Purchase Agreement

It is perhaps the most common type of contract that may have to deal in the world of real estate. This contract comprises of all the details regarding the sale of the property. It includes information such as the address of the property, names of both parties, price, signatures of the parties involved, and the closing date of the deal.

There are further three classifications of purchase agreements, which are:

1. **State/Association purchase agreement:** A standard agreement between a buyer and a seller when a real estate agent is involved in the deal.
2. **General Purchase Agreement:** A contract

agreement directly between the buyer and the seller with no involvement of a real estate agent.

3. **Commercial Agreement:** This type of agreement involves commercial property/land.

Real Estate Assignment Contract

This type of contract is often used in a wholesale investment purchase. This might include a distressed property that is secure and then assigned to a different buyer. This contract comprises of terms such as "assigns" which is used to differentiate it as an assignment contract.

Residential Lease Agreement

This type of contract is used for binding an owner and a renter of the property. By signing this contract, the owner of the property agrees with a tenant to reside in the property at pre-defined monthly rent. Some additional items can also be included in this contract, such as payment of the utility bills and also the security deposit. It is very important to ensure that all the items are added in the lease agreement to prevent legal disputes in the future.

In Florida, we also often use the form "Contract to Lease" to present the offer. The important thing to note here is that this contract to lease is not actually a lease; instead, it is just a method of presenting an offer and after negotiation of the terms becomes a "Residential Lease." The Residential Lease should be signed before occupancy and should have the same terms that were negotiated on the contract to lease. Contract to lease is intended to be a legally binding contract, and it has a definite date for executing a lease agreement.

Power of Attorney

Generally, a power of attorney is not used in the real estate contracts. However, some cases allow it if a party is unable to sign the contract themselves. For example, if a party is not physically present in the country to sign the contract on their own, then they can hire another party to act as their power of attorney to sign on their behalf.

A power of attorney can also be quite useful if a party involves people who are suffering from any mental or physical illness, which prevents them from signing the contract. Old age is also one of the factors that allow it.

A power of attorney comes in handy when a foreigner is not in the country at the moment of the closing and sends a representative (power of attorney), any person who the client trusts enough to sign the contract on their behalf. Most of the times, the responsibilities of the "power of attorney" are pretty limited as they only involve the sale/purchase of a specific property.

Understanding the contracts is also incredibly beneficial for your personal progress towards becoming a top producer in the real estate industry. Sometimes you will have to deal with customers who have no knowledge regarding the contracts. Therefore, it would be really helpful for them if you could guide them in this area as well. You will not only gain the client's trust, but your reputation will also receive a much-needed boost.

Once you have learned everything there is to learn regarding the world of the real estate, it doesn't mean that your training has ended. The real industry is vast and full of challenges. You will have to deal with different kinds of clients and learn so many things as your progress along the way. In fact, you will be in training all your career because there are so many things that you will only be able to learn through experience and not through a training class. The real estate landscape is continuously changing, and you have to evolve with all those changes.

Chapter 4

Marketing

"Real estate cannot be lost or stolen, nor can it be carried away. Purchased with common sense, paid for in full, and managed with reasonable care, it is about the safest investment in the world."

- *Franklin D. Roosevelt (32nd U.S President)*

Marketing is one of the most important aspects of every business strategy in the world. You are not going to sell your product and services if people aren't even aware of your existence. The same theory applies when we talk about the real estate business.

Marketing is a simple way to attract customers by advertising your products and services to them. In real estate perspective, people are always looking for a suitable property to buy, sell, or lease. However, since most of them lack essential knowledge in this area, they look for trusted brokers to make the deals on their behalf. Another major reason why most people tend to look for brokers is that they have valuable connections with other buyers and sellers and can get them a good deal.

So how do you market yourself as a top producer in the real estate world? As a real estate expert, people always ask me this question, and my answer is through the combination of traditional and modern marketing techniques.

By traditional marketing techniques, I mean utilizing

old school methods such as newspaper ads, yellow pages, postcards, milk carton ads, etc. Modern methods mean utilizing the internet, social media, email marketing, and many others.

I believe marketing is a non-stop process, and I must have at least eight leads in my hand at all times. Having any lead, whether they are buyers, sellers, or renters, is important. It makes sure that you do not have to sit idly by when the market is going down. Any lead is a great opportunity to help you expand and also grow your business.

A top producer is always marketing themselves even by how they carry themselves. You should be dressed well and look decent all the time so that when you meet potential customers at any social gathering, they take you seriously. Always talk about your business in all social gatherings or events because you never know when you can get a customer. Real estate investment is an interesting topic, and it mostly grabs people's attention as it is a money making option for them.

Here are some of the tips that you can use to get the customers:

1. Spread the Word to Your Friends and Family

One of the easiest and most basic ways of marketing is by spreading the word regarding your business through friends and family. People who you trust the most are more likely going to help you out in this area even without any expected compensation. They can casually inform their social circle about your business and get you some customers just like that.

2. Get on Social Media

The world of internet is as vast as it can get in today's world and it is expanding every second. One of the biggest opportunities to lure new customers is through social media. Businesses who ignore social media platforms tend to miss out on massive opportunities and often lose to their competitors. People expect you to be on any social media channel; otherwise, they are disappointed in the services.

As a real estate top producer, you need to make sure that you are present on all of the major social media channels such as Facebook, Twitter, Instagram, Reddit, and many others.

One of the main advantages of social media marketing is that it is very cheap. In fact, it can also be free if you know how to use it effectively. You can gain a lot of followers by sharing interesting content from your account. After you have gathered a healthy amount of followers, you can start spreading the word about your real estate business and ask your loyal followers to help you out.

Another way to get potential customers on social media platform is through ad services and promotional services of the platforms. These services are relatively cheaper than all the other advertisement options out there on the internet. By utilizing these services, you can target a specific type of audience who are most likely to avail your services.

3. Get a Killer Business Card

Business cards are certainly not a new marketing concept. It has been around for ages, and it is still pretty much effective. Sure emails, social media, and online messages are pretty effective to some effect. However, they do not have the physicality that a business card offers because it can be held in your hand physically.

To make your business card effective, make sure it has a unique and attractive design. The more attractive your business card, the better the impact it's going to make on your potential customers.

Make sure to keep the content on your business card as minimal as possible. It should only contain important information such as your name, profession, firm's name, and your contact information. I also suggest people put their social media and website address on the business card as well as it shows you are well caught up with the times.

Hand out your business card to every person you meet, whether it is for a social gathering or a professional one. Also, distribute it among your friends and family and ask them to give it away to their social circle.

4. Create A Killer Website

This is probably the most obvious step that I shouldn't even be discussing here. However, many people are running big businesses and still do not have any online presence. In today's day and age, an online presence is a must. That's because the internet has completely taken over the world. The first thing that any typical person does when looking for anything is going to search bar (Google, Yahoo, or Bing) and type it out. If you do not have any website, then you lose out to the competition.

A website is like a private place or office that the users can visit from the comfort of their homes. They can explore and find out about services, and in the end, decide to buy your products or services. As a real estate agent, you can set your website up as a way of getting in touch with potential clients by showing them your portfolio and successful reputation.

Of course, anyone can create a website. It's that easy nowadays. There are hundreds of millions of active websites out there, but not all of them are as effective. You need to make sure that your website stands out among the competition. To do that, you may need to hire a professional to design and develop your website. You also need to place high-quality content on the website that is both informative and persuasive. The website should be easy to use and also mobile-friendly since most of the people today access the internet through their mobile devices.

5. Start Blogging

So you have created a great website. But the work isn't finished here. You need to promote your website so that your potential customers can find it easily online.

One of the best ways to promote your website is by creating a blog and updating it daily. Make sure to add high-quality content, including pictures and videos of the properties that are available to be purchased or sold. Another thing you need to take care of is to use relevant keywords. Using specific keywords help your website rank higher on the search results and enables the users to find it easily.

6. Lookout for Your Competitors

The most important people that you need to look out for are none other than your competitors. If they are beating you, then you need to check out their strategies. How is their website? How do they deal with the customers on social media platforms? What kind of ads are they creating to attract the customers? After checking out all of their strategies, work out how you can make it better to attract the customers towards your services.

7. Hire A Professional Photographer

This tip might seem a bit weird to you, but it is quite important. If you can afford to, then you should hire a professional photographer to work with you. That's because you need to have high-quality content for your website and social media profiles to attract potential customers. Ask your photographer to capture exquisite photos of the properties that you are trying to get purchased or sold. Then use these images on your ads, website, and social media platforms.

Similarly, you can also utilize your photographer to record a high-quality video to create a video tour of the property that you can upload on video-specific social media channels such as YouTube.

8. Send Newsletters Through Emails

Email marketing is still one of the best and most effective marketing techniques for building strong client relationships. All you have to do is collect email addresses of your potential clients. You can do this through the email subscription service on your website, your local outreach, or any other methods. After you are done with collecting the lists, you can start sending them what they are seeking. It could be information about the upcoming open houses, new houses on the market, particularly real estate news about the area that you work in, etc.

Note: If you work in different geographical locations, then you should segment your newsletters accordingly. Make sure people living in certain areas only receive information regarding their areas.

9. Send Postcards

Postcards are one of the old fashioned marketing strategies that are still pretty effective today. It is a great way to make your customers, and potential customers feel special so that they come back to you the next time as well.

Many realtors use postcards as a marketing tool to promote new open houses, share a new listing, or even thank a customer for a referral.

Just like business cards, a postcard is also a tangible item. This means that people are most likely to pass it around as referrals. According to a study conducted by the National Association of Realtors (NAR), 89 percent of buyers choose their agent again or at least recommend them to others[1].

Here are some of the postcard ideas that you use to market your real estate services:

- **Postcards for Buyers and Sellers:** Specially designed postcards that market your buying or selling services.
- **Rental Postcard:** You can design and send postcards that market a particular place or several properties available for rent.
- **Agent Postcard:** A postcard designed for marketing agency services.
- **Appreciation Postcard:** A thank you postcard that you can send to your loyal customers who helped you out with referral(s).

---

[1]National Association of Realtors (2018). Quick Real Estate Statistics: https://www.nar.realtor/research-and-statistics/quick-real-estate-statistics

- **Holiday Postcard:** A holiday greeting card is a great way to market your services.

10. Use Online Ad Services

Marketing is a business. To gain something, you need to lose something. Working on your website and social media channels extensively is pretty effective. However, it doesn't happen overnight and takes days and sometimes even months before your potential clients start seeing you online. There is, however, a quicker way to the top, but it requires some money. It's the online ad services.

There are many advertisement options available on the internet that you can use for your own advantage. You can either go for PPC (Pay-Per-Click) ads on search engines or social media ads that appear on some of the most popular platforms in the world.

These ads straightforwardly target your desired audience and give you quick results when compared to the conventional ways. However, it all comes down to how attractive or persuasive your ad is to compel the users to click on it and make a purchase.

11. Brand Yourself

Let's imagine a silhouette of a bitten apple, what's the first thing that comes to your mind? The most likely answer would be the tech giant Apple Inc. This is the effect of branding. As a real estate agent, you also need to make a brand of yourself or your agency. You can do that by creating a logo with a particular text that stands out.

You can use this brand image on your business cards, postcards, letterheads, and also print it out on pens, cups, and other goodies that you can hand out to your potential customers. This is a great marketing technique that has proven to be effective time and time again.

12. Partner with Local Businesses

Another effective way to advertise your services among the local community is by partnering with the local businesses. You can get them to sell merchandise with your logo on them along with contact details of your services. You can also sponsor local events and distribute pamphlets and business cards in return.

13. Get on Zillow

Zillow is an online real estate database company that can also be considered as the Yelp of real estate marketing. Every real estate agent has to create an account on Zillow; otherwise, they are missing out on a massive opportunity.

Zillow is a pretty trustworthy website, and it accounts for almost 48 percent of all site traffic for real estate searches on the web. It also offers a great opportunity for you to advertise yourself as an agent on their website. This service certainly isn't cheap, but it is worth it.

14. Request for Reviews

One thing that you need to take care of online are the reviews. The reviews are pretty much your evaluation report that potential customers see to decide whether they should go for your services or not. You need to make sure that your business has great reviews on large platforms such as Google and Yelp.

One way to do it is by requesting your most satisfied customers to add positive reviews online. In this way, you will be able to maintain a good reputation and also attract many other customers.

15.Stay In Touch

One of the best ways to make sure that clients return to you next time is by keeping in touch with them. Make sure to get all the contact information of your clients even if they intend on availing your services once only. Keep in touch with them by sending them anniversary cards, holiday cards and inform them about new offers. Also, keep on requesting for a referral. In this way, you will always be on top of their minds whenever they think about contacting a real estate agent.

Marketing is just the way to deliver a message to your prospect regarding your real estate services. You need to present yourself as the primary expert in a specific neighborhood. That's because the first thing you need to do is conquer your area and then move on to the next one. You should have complete knowledge about the area that you are working in, such as the locations of local banks, stores, and restaurants. Knowing your area makes you look like a well-qualified realtor, and people are more likely to trust you.

Chapter 5

What Should I Do When I Receive a Call from a Potential Customer?

"Your customers are the lifeblood of your business. Their needs and wants impact every aspect of your business, from product development to content marketing to sales to customer service."

- *John Rampton*

So you have mastered the marketing techniques necessary to promote your real estate business. A successful marketing campaign means that people will develop an interest in acquiring your services. Therefore, you should be mentally prepared to turn these potential customers into your actual customers. One of the most primary means of communication that prospects are going to use to contact you is the phone. So, one question might come into your mind at this point, and that is, what should I do when I receive a call from a potential customer? Well, this chapter will answer this question in intricate details.

As a real estate agent myself, whenever a customer contacts me to inquire about my services, the first thing I do is schedule a face-to-face meeting with them. The reason I do that is that a personal meeting is much more useful than talking to someone on the phone or through an internet chat. Don't get me wrong, technology is amazing, and it has made our lives much easier when it comes to marketing and communication. But nothing beats an old fashioned face-to-face communication.

Just to prove my point, here are some of the benefits of a face-to-face meeting with your potential customer:

- **Easier to convince people:** Since the person you are talking to will be giving you their full attention, it is much easier to convince them during a face-to-face meeting. Talking with them over the phone or chat does not get you the same attention, and it is much harder to prove your point this way.
- **Shows body language:** According to many studies, 90 percent of human communication comprises of body language. Therefore, people are better able to understand each other in a personal meeting.
- **Values the other person:** When you value someone, you take out time from your busy schedule to meet them. A potential customer is more likely to appreciate this effort, and it may convince them easily as well.
- **Develops trust:** Talking over phone or chat doesn't show your tone or body language at all. It is hard to trust a person you have never met before behind the curtains. Face-to-face meetings fill this void and help you build a trustworthy relationship with your customers.

I am sure all of these benefits have enlightened your perspective on face-to-face meetings. However, it is isn't that easy to set up personal meetings in today's busy world. A lot of your potential customers will likely avoid a personal meeting simply because either they are too busy to do so or don't want to lose the comfort of talking from their rooms. Therefore, to convince them for a meeting is another challenge. Find a suitable time for the meeting and make sure it is convenient for both you and your prospect. In this way, both of you will be able to give each other full attention. Of course, this won't always happen immediately. It can sometimes take days before you can agree on a date and time to meet.

Whenever you receive a call from a potential customer, the first thing you need to do is give a brief introduction about yourself and the company you are working for. Make sure to include all your major accolades in this introduction as well, such as "we provide the best real estate services in the San Francisco Bay Area."

The next thing you need to do after the greetings and introduction is to ask them about the services they are looking for. Usually, if the customer is contacting you, then they will tell you themselves. However, it is just a nice gesture to ask them politely what they want.

There are three primary services in the world of real estate that a customer might be looking for:

- Buying
- Selling
- Renting

You need to figure out which service your customer is seeking to prepare yourself mentally. That's because all three of these services are different and require different methods to deal with the customers.

I have separated all three of these services to provide you with a clear perspective of how to deal with potential clients.

How to Deal with Buyers?

If a customer contacts you and tells you that they are looking to purchase a property, then you need to ask them about all the details of their requirement. You need to ask them about what kind of property they are looking for, what should be the size of the place, in what price range, etc. In this way, you will be able to filter them out early.

To make sure your deal stays firm with the potential client, you need to educate them right away. A lot of deals fall through because the customer starts having doubts and worries midway. That's because they are unsure about a lot of things and you are the person to make sure they do. Provide your customers with an early education regarding the problems that they might face and how to deal with them.

I have prepared a list of things that you can tell your buyer clients to educate them beforehand of a deal:

1. Lowest Price Means No Concessions

It is an absolute dream scenario for every buyer to purchase a property at the lowest price possible. If you somehow manage to get your buyer the best bargain by bringing the seller to the rock bottom price, then you need to tell the buyers to expect no concessions. Usually, if sellers get a good price for their property, they tend to offer certain concessions such as repair work or minor renovation of the property. However, they will not agree on providing such services if they are beaten on the price. Therefore, you need to make sure that the buyers are aware of this scenario before closing the deal to avoid future confusions or dispute.

2. A Really Low Offer Can Backfire

When the market is slowing down a bit, buyers can sometimes be motivated to make some ridiculously low offers for the property. You need to warn your buyer clients not to do that as it can backfire. A low offer can drive the sellers to make a high counter offer, which can raise the price more than the list price, and the buyers end up paying more than they should.

Sometimes, a really low offer can offend the sellers as well, and they might even straightforwardly refuse to sell the property to that particular buyer. Therefore, you need to inform your clients regarding this situation as well.

3. Always Do Comparative Analysis

If one of your buyer clients shows interest in a property, then they are going to ask you a simple question, "How much should I pay for this property?" At this point, uttering out the price of the property might not be a good idea. So, you should do a comparative analysis in front of them to generate an idea in their minds. Tell them about the recently sold properties in the same area. Once they get the idea and you feel like they are interested in buying the property, then you can go ahead and reveal the price.

4. I'm Not Expert in All Things, But I Can Help You Locate One

It pays off to be an expert in all things in today's world. However, you should stay out of the areas that you lack in expertise. A lot of real estate brokers and agents get into troubles when trying to help their clients where they really shouldn't. Keep one thing in mind: you are a real estate expert, not a lawyer, not an engineer, and not an inspector. Whenever any task for any of these professions is required during the deal, you should answer that you don't know. However, you should have contact with people of these professions just for the convenience of your clients.

5. Don't Buy New Furniture Until After the Deal is Closed

A lot of customers get excited when they are getting near to closing a deal. Some of them even go out shopping for furniture for their new home. However, you should warn your customers not to do so until after closing the deal. That's because, sometimes, a seller can back out from the deal at the last moment and there is simply nothing you can do about that.

That is all you need to know when dealing with clients that are willing to pay for the property with cash. However, you need to ask these clients for proof of funds.

You will also most likely meet some clients that will be willing to purchase the property on a mortgage. A mortgage is simply an agreement with the bank where it lends the money to people in exchange for taking the title of the debtor's property. After the payment is completed, the conveyance of the title becomes void.

There is a different way to deal with mortgage clients. These are some of the things that you need to ask the clients that are planning to buy the property on mortgage:

A. Ask Them How Much They Can Borrow

This is really important information as it provides you with the perspective of the range of the property that your client might be able to afford. This depends on how much monthly payment can your client afford. A lender decides this based on the credit and employment history, debt situation, and income of the client. You can advise your client to consult a loan officer to acquire this information if they haven't already.

B. Ask Them If They Are Pre-Qualified

Another important thing that you need to ask your client is if they are prequalified for a mortgage purchase or not. A prequalification determines whether an individual is worthy of borrowing the loan from a lender.

You can guide your client through the prequalification process. With their permission, a loan officer can pull their credit report, which helps them prequalify for financing. You can then use your client's prequalification to make the best offer on the property of your client's choice.

How to Deal with Sellers?

Dealing with the clients that are looking to sell their property means working on the opposite side of the spectrum. You need to change your perspective entirely and view the whole situation from the seller's point of view. Many agents simultaneously work for the buyers and sellers on the same deal.

The first thing you need to do when dealing with the seller client is to help them arrange a listing presentation. This means that both of you need to arrange a meeting to do that. This will give you the chance to explain to them how you plan to sell their property.

Here are some of the things that you need to do as a real estate agent when dealing with seller clients:

1. Price the Property Correctly

The ideal scenario for every seller is to sell their property way higher than the listed price. As a good real estate agent, you should always list the property on the right price. A lot of real estate agents tend to overprice the property to earn a seller client. This is ethically wrong.

Pricing a property way too high may drive away from the buyers. It can also develop a bad reputation in the market, which makes it difficult to sell it. The price should always be listed close to the actual market price.

2. Market the Property

A good marketing method will sell almost anything on this planet. It is one area where your real estate skills are tested, especially when you are working with a seller client. Take great pictures of the property and send them to the potential buyers. You can also post these pictures on real estate websites such as Zillow and also social media accounts to attract other buyers.

3. Communicate Properly

Proper communication is also one of the most important aspects of dealing with seller clients. If someone is trusting you with the selling of their property, then you need to ensure that they have chosen the right person for the job. One to do it is by constantly updating them regarding every situation.

A lot of real estate agents only contact their seller clients whenever there is an offer. This means that if there's no offer for months, they won't contact them for the entire time. You need to keep updating the clients to give the impression that you are doing your best to sell their property for the right price. Inform them about showings and interest from potential buyers.

One of the biggest complaints about the real estate agents is that they lack proper communication. So, you need to make sure you fill this void and stand out among the others.

4. Negotiate the Best Terms

A great real estate agent fights hard for the best terms and conditions for their clients. You should never worry about what will go into your own pockets but how much of a good deal of it would be for your client. This helps you develop a good reputation in the industry, and clients are most likely to come back to you or refer you to others.

I hope the points I have shared with you here have provided with a proper insight on how to properly deal with the seller clients. To give an example of the real-life scenario, I have shared some conversations below to help you further understand the interaction of a realtor and a seller client:

Objection: In a listing presentation Seller JOE wants to sell their home by themselves (they do not want to pay commissions)

Joe: We want to sell our house, but we are going to do it by ourselves, we already have an FSBO sign in place.

Realtor: I understand you, and realize that you want to get the maximum amount of money for your sale, right?

Joe: Right.

Realtor: What if I show you that selling the property through me you will get more money and you will also be able to sell it faster? Will you be interested in that? Selling is a numbers game. We have certain marketing methods that will make every realtor aware of your home's existence. People that come through a realtor are already pre-approved by a lender. They are not just curious people who waste your time. When you do it yourself, you can expect people to come knocking on your door at any time of the day or calling you in the middle of the night. How do you feel safe opening the door to strangers and answering their questions ANY hour? Well, I do that for a living. I answer all these questions, and I also ask for pre-approvals. I show them the properties and close the deal by selling them the house. I am going to sell your house for you in the same way. Now let me ask one question, when I sell your house, where would you move to? I can also help you with purchasing your next home. I can start showing you properties right away!

Important Note: Always carry an exclusive right to sell property agreement when you go to listings presentations!

Objection: Seller is ready to give you the listing, but he says that he is negotiating with a neighbor the sale of the house and he needs a couple of days to see what is going to happen.

Realtor: Ok, I fully understand you, what is the name of the neighbor? What we can do here is write an addendum that if this specific neighbor buys the property then I will not be a part of the deal and you won't owe my company any fees or commission nor me. Sounds fair, right? Let's sign the agreement, so I can start working for you.

Objection: Seller wants to negotiate your commission and that you only earn let's say 1%.

Joe: I will only sign if you collect only 1 % as a listing agent and 3 % for a Buyer agent.

Realtor: I understand you, but you need to think of the big numbers. I will have to do a lot of work when it comes to marketing your house. I will do everything that it takes to sell your property at the right price. My main goal is to get more money for you and not negotiating my earned commission. Remember that I will negotiate your selling price the same way that I'm negotiating my commission. Sounds fair? Let's sign the agreement, so I can start working for you.

Objection: FSBO says, "Bring me a buyer, and I will give you 3% commission."

Realtor: I understand your position, now you need to understand that we have our search engines where we search for properties for our customers, right? Your property is currently not listed there, and I am the person to list it there. Once it is listed, then it will be visible to all the other realtors.

You are not marketing your property unless people see it. If I work for you, many more people will be aware that you are selling the property. Remember that this is a number's game.

Joe: Yes, I understand what you are saying, but I also believe that I can find a person on my own that can buy my property. If it's a realtor, I will honor the 3% commission.

Realtor: Ok, I understand that just wondering, if someone comes here right now to buy the property and both of you agree on the price and other items, what will you do next? What contract are you going to sign? Will it have a mortgage or cash? Do you understand all the contract clauses? Which Title Company will you use?

Let me help you in the process of selling the house with a good marketing strategy. We will have more customers willing to buy your property. You understand that by average the property sold by a realtor net more money than FSBO, right?

When we sell your property, where are you moving to? Let me help you with your next purchase. (Always ask this).

Objection: The Market price of the property is $250K, but I want $300K for it because my house has marble floors and a nice pool.

Realtor: I understand what you are saying. When do you need your home to be sold? Where are you moving to?

Joe: I need it to be sold right away, and I want to move to this other neighborhood which I looked on the internet, they have very good prices.

Realtor: Great! But first understand this, there's a market price on every market, prices go up and down according to demand. Now, the neighborhood you mentioned is very similar to this one. We can list your property and wait to be sold. It can take days or even months. When we sell it for your price normally, the other neighborhood prices were going to be up as well. I can show you the prices of similar properties in that area. Let's see if we can reach a price that can be good for you and you can move to the other neighborhood.

Script for (Sales) on the Internet

Customer: Is this available?

Agent: Yes

Agent: Is this purchase for investment or living?

Questions like these are just to "break the ice" and to start gathering information.

Agent: Will it be a cash purchase, or you need financing? We can also help you get a mortgage if you need. If needed call (your Loan Officer Name and phone #)

Customer: It will be for living, and it will be a cash offer.

Agent: Perfect! Do you want to see it tomorrow at 4 pm? I can arrange a visit at that time. We can meet at our office at 3:30 pm and go from there. I also have other options with similar characteristics.

Customer: Great, this is ok for me. Where is your office located?

Agent: (your brokerage name and address)

Agent: Please provide your phone # for confirmation.

Customer: (305) xxx-xxxx

Agent: Perfect, see you tomorrow at 4pm.

Important Note: *Normally we do not know the visiting time, we tell the customer a random time 24 hours after talking with him/her and then we can re-schedule.*

How to Deal with Clients Looking for Tenancy Agreements?

Not all realtors deal with clients looking for rental properties. Some of them tend to do it on the side. But it depends on the location. Cities like New York or San Francisco, where there's a huge population of renters, it is quite common for realtors to deal with the rental clients.

As a good real estate agent, you should be able to find your rental clients the ideal place that they are seeking. Of course, this means that you should be aware of all the right properties that are listed for rent only.

A lot of people tend to look for rental properties on their own. If you tend to find such potential client, then you should educate them regarding the advantages of hiring a realtor to find a rental property. You should tell them that you will guide them from scratch and you will help them find what they are looking for and also at the right price.

You should also inform them that a realtor will take on all the hassles, such as tracking down the landlord and property managers and dealing with them on your client's behalf. A realtor can also help them negotiate terms mentioned on the lease. Sometimes, a lease has all kinds of vital information such as repairs the renter would be responsible for, the penalties for late rent and terms and conditions for breaking a lease. If a client is inexperienced, then they can easily fall victim by signing a bad lease. A good realtor can help them prevent it.

Here is a script I have prepared to show you the conversation between a customer, who is looking to rent a property and a real estate agent:

Customer: Is this property available for rent?

Agent: Yes.

Agent: When do you need to move?

If the customer says in 2 or 3 months, it is better to tell them that what we are going to send them now as it might not be available in 3 months and that it is better to start 45 days before.

If the customer says, "right away," we cannot show any place with Associations as by average it takes 3 to 4 weeks to approve, can be a Single home or Rental Community.

Customer: As soon as possible.

Agent: Perfect, the association on this unit takes around three weeks for approval.

Agent: can you come to our _____ (Brokerage city) office tomorrow at 10am so we can see this unit and others with similar characteristics?

If the customer says YES, send the office address / If NOT ask when it could be a good time to come.

After you schedule a time for the meeting at the office ask for Phone #

Agent: Please provide me your phone # for Confirmation.

If the customer provides a phone # send a text confirming the meeting (and to make sure this is the correct phone #) if the customer doesn't provide the phone number, the meeting is not confirmed.

Important Note: *Remember that by average the rental price has to be on third of total income.*

If a tenant earns $6000 per month, rental has to be $2000 or lower.

Always remember that it is easy to get a customer, and much harder to retain one. Whenever I receive a renter, they are usually unaware of their ability to purchase the house. Making them reach this realization is up to you, and you can help them see the benefits of purchasing a house. Certain questions can allow you to evaluate whether or not customers will purchase a property in the future.

Chapter 6

I've Talked to the Customer, Now What?

"It's not about the money, though that's nice to have. At the end of the day, it's really about matching the right buyer to the right seller. We're matchmakers – real estate matchmakers."

- *Valerie Fitzgerald*

After going through challenging marketing techniques, hopefully, you will be able to land some clients. These potential customers are going to contact you through phone call or any other communication medium. What you should do next is thoroughly explained in the previous chapter. However, the very first thing that I recommended there was to set up a meeting immediately.

Arranging a meeting might seem like an easy task, and it is in some instances. However, it can be a big headache when you are dealing with an extremely busy client. Finding free time out of their occupied schedule is a nightmare situation, and doing it can be considered as an achievement.

In some cases, the client will straightforwardly refuse to meet at all. There could be many reasons for their refusals. They could be just buying the property for investment purpose and don't even care to look at it themselves, or they could be some foreign investors who are looking to invest in the country while sitting in their home.

One solution for dealing with such clients is to ask them if they can send a representative for themselves to look at the properties on their behalf. If that is out of the question as well, then you will have to do all the work by yourself and make sure you do your best to satisfy these clients.

I would like to suggest that you should have all the information regarding the listed properties beforehand. It helps you in cases like these. Even if you are not doing any work for a client, you should be visiting newly listed properties to have a look and collect all the necessary information about it. You should also collect images and videos of the property to keep it as a record for future prospects. This allows you to immediately present the available options to clients that refuse to meet. You can send them information through the mail, email, or any other form of communication to give them a review of the property.

If the clients choose one of the properties that you sent them, that's a jackpot for you. You will have the chance to instantly close the deal without even getting out of your office. If they don't like any of those, then you need to take out a pen and paper and start asking them details regarding what they are seeking. You should ask them each and everything about the area they want to buy, sell, or rent the property in. What kind of price range they are expecting and also what kind of property they are after. After noting down all the details, you need to filter these requirements from your current collected data. If you find it there, then that's brilliant. If you don't, then it is time to get back out on the field.

Since your potential client is unable to make it to the showing themselves, you will have to do the work on their behalf. You can look for their specific properties on the realtors' search engines or ask your fellow realtors if they happen to know about such properties. After finding out the ideal properties, you need to visit them and make sure that they are exactly what the remote client is seeking. I recommend (again) to take vivid photos (and videos if it helps) of the property so that you can send it to the prospects.

You should visit all the properties that match the criteria defined by the clients. After collecting the results, send them to the clients and ask them to make a decision and contact you then. Some of them may ask for some time to think, and you should definitely allow them. Never pressurize to hurry up on a decision. However, you should inform them about the fact that other people might also be looking at the same properties, and if they don't make the first bid, someone else surely will.

As your clients think and make a decision, you can get back to dealing with your other clients in the meantime. But, your work with the remote client isn't finished yet. The next thing you need to do is follow-up.

After waiting for a few days, you need to contact your remote clients and politely ask them if they had made any decision over the past few days. If they ask for some more time to think, you should remind them again that the property that they choose might not be available forever. It would be better to make the decision quickly.

If one of your clients finally comes up with the decision and chooses a certain property to proceed with, then you should again ask for a face-to-face meeting with them if possible. The reason I am emphasizing a lot on the meeting is because of all the benefits that I mentioned in the previous chapter. If they somehow agree for the meeting now, then it is great. Otherwise, you will have to work on behalf of them again and proceed towards closing the deal.

The real estate is a pretty tricky industry, especially when it comes to the type of clients that you meet here. Not all of them are easy ones. By easy, I mean experienced buyers and sellers who know how things work. These people take their time and understand the delays if they happen. They are also straightforward and don't create any hassle during the closing of the deal.

The world is full of unique individuals. Every person on this planet is different from the other. Therefore, you should be ready to face any client in this business.

Throughout my career as a realtor, I have dealt with all kinds of clients. Some of them were so easy to work with while some of them gave sleepless nights. Just to give you an insight into what you could expect, I have prepared a list of challenging clients that you will most likely meet as a realtor:

1. First-Time Buyers

One of the most difficult clients to deal with are first-time buyers. These are the people that are in need for the most guidance from your side. It depends on the type of person they are. Some of the newbies will accept their lack of knowledge in the area and will follow your lead quietly, while some of them may wake you up every night at 3 am only to ask a ridiculous question. However, you must deal with them in the best way possible, you might end up with a repeat client.

Many issues arise with first-time buyers. One of them is their choices of properties. For example, one client might look at a really expensive property on the internet that well exceeds their budget, and demand that you help them buy it. It is your job to politely educate them about the market value of the properties and how it varies in price from area-to-area.

Usually, first-time buyers are a little overwhelmed and can easily get lost in the process. You should help them by asking them to outline their priorities. The priorities should comprise of their preferred area, budget, and any other thing they are seeking.

The next thing you should do is prepare your own to-do list. By looking at their outline, you can decide how many properties match the criteria. After sorting everything out, you can take them for showings.

2. Big Dreamers with Small Wallets

These types of clients know what they are seeking. The only problem is, they don't have the cash to achieve their dreams. They have difficulty to accept the reality of their budget, and they require serious guidance in this area, and you have to be the voice of reason for them.

There is nothing wrong in dreaming big. This country was built around the concept of the "American Dream." However, we also need to accept the reality that some things are simply out of our reach. To deal with such clients, you need to stick to the same approach that you use with first-time buyers. Ask them to outline their priorities. Next, ask them to make some compromise on the outline according to their budget. If they refuse any compromise, then you have to be blunt and tell them that they cannot afford what they are asking for. Offer to show them properties that fall under their budget.

3. The 'Know-All' Clients

Another type of clients that you will most likely meet as a realtor are the overly enthusiastic people that claim to know everything about real estate. These are the people that have watched pretty much every show on the HGTV and think they know everything required for buying a property.

Surprisingly, some of these people do have a lot of knowledge regarding how real estate deals work. This can be helpful for realtors. However, their overconfidence can sometimes get in your way of working, so you need to be careful when dealing with them.

If a client is excited to buy a property, then you should support their enthusiasm. However, you should also know when to act as a facilitator and when to transform into an authoritative figure. They might know a lot, but they sure don't know as much as you do. You should make sure that you lead them through the process on YOUR terms. Once your job is done, and the deal is closed, they should be free to take over from there.

4. The Attention Seekers

These clients are action-oriented and laser-focused people. They don't realize that you have other clients as well and demand your complete attention every single time.

This type of client will constantly disturb you with meaningless calls, text messages, and emails. Their eagerness can become a serious obstacle in your work, and you may even have difficulty finding what they are looking for.

The best way to deal with such clients is to be blunt with them. Stay clear of promises of when can they expect a response from you. If you cannot reply to their dozens of messages and emails, then send them a message only when your schedule allows it. Be truthful about your busy schedule and tell them that they are only making things difficult due to their constant disturbance.

Handling clients with different personalities has always been a major challenge for realtors. However, the more prepared the agent is for all of these different people, the better he/she will be able to handle them.

My ultimate tip here is that whenever you encounter a difficult client, take a step back and identify the type of client you are dealing with. Once you have analyzed it, then react accordingly. By adapting to the needs of a client, you are just demonstrating your incredible set of skills as a real estate agent. You need to make sure that you are seen as an ally by them and not an obstacle.

Chapter 7

Negotiating the Terms

"In the real estate business, you learn more about people, you learn more about community issues, you learn more about life, you learn more about the impact of government, probably more than any other profession that I know of."

- *Johnny Isakson*

A top producer should possess sharp negotiation skills. You are conducting a business, and you deserve a fair share for your contribution.

After the customer has decided on purchasing, selling, or renting a property, the next most important thing you need to do is prepare an offer and get them to sign it. I like to do this personally. After getting the signatures, you must send the offer to the listing agent so they can update the status of the property and you don't receive any more offers.

Just to be on the safe side, I always recommend getting your contract double-checked by your broker. In this way, you can point out any shortcomings or unnecessary clauses in the contracts and adjust them accordingly.

To commence negotiations on a positive note, it is better to ask the buyer to submit some funds through escrow. It sends a message to the seller that you are interested in closing the deal. If the deal is for renting a property, then you should ask the tenant to submit one month's rent in advance through escrow. If it's a purchase, then somewhere between 1 and 5 percent of purchase price should be submitted to escrow.

After your funds have transferred into the escrow account, you should send the offer to the brokerage within three business days. It is better to attach proof of funds with the offer if the customer is paying in cash. You can also attach a preapproval letter if you have taken out a loan.

The offer contract should also have a deadline. The seller must have a final date to respond. If the seller fails to respond within that particular time limit, then the contract is voided. It would present good news for the buyer if they made their payments through escrow. They receive their payment from escrow in case the seller stays unresponsive for a long time.

The seller may respond to the offer in three different ways:

1) They reject it.

2) They accept it.

3) They make a counteroffer.

The first two options are straightforward. But if you receive a counteroffer from the seller, then you must inform the buyer. They can make a sound decision based on the seller's counteroffer.

A counter offer is just a part of the negotiation process. It is not the final price. There is always room for negotiation until the seller says otherwise.

Once a contract is executed, you should send an email to both the buyer and the seller stating the execution date of the contract. Deliver a copy of the executed contract to the brokerage, the mortgage company and the company that holds title to the property.

The next thing you need to do is set a reminder for all contingencies. For example, there is an inspection in ten days, or renovation work is due next week, etc. Make sure that your client is aware of all contingencies.

Keep the following contingencies in mind:

1. Inspection

I always recommend buyers to use the "special inspection contingency" clause in the contract instead of the "general" one. It is every buyer's right to have the property inspected by a professional inspection company. You must request a satisfactory inspection before closing the purchase.

Most buyers tend to sign contracts right away, without ever thinking about an inspection. At the time of closing the deal, their sole focus lies on moving into the new home and finding the perfect place to call home. They tend to overlook contingencies like inspections. As a result, they miss out on any faults that the property could have. Once they have signed the contract and made the purchase, an inspection only informs them of the expenses they will surely incur because of a neglected fault. If they had opted for inspection before purchase, maybe they would have avoided buying such a property.

Now let's discuss differences between general and special inspection contingencies. In a general contingency, if the buyer is dissatisfied with the inspection results, they can terminate the contract. Their deposited funds are refunded to them.

In a special inspection, the buyers may agree to buy

the property conditionally by adding an extra clause in the contract. For example, if the inspection results show too many faults in the property, then the buyer may allow three days to the seller so they can agree to make the repairs. After the seller responds, the buyer gets two additional days to decide whether they accept what the seller has offered to do.

2. Appraisal

A real estate contract contains appraisal contingency that protects buyers. It is there to ensure that the property is valued at a minimum specified amount depending on its list price in the market. If the property fails to appraise for at least the specified amount, then the contract can be terminated. In many cases, the buyer gets a full refund.

In some cases, even when the value of the property, as per the appraisal, is lower than the specified amount, the buyer may be willing to close the deal. In this case, it is up to the seller to decide whether they would sell at the appraised value or the offered value. The buyer receives the notice of appraisal value within a specified number of days. After receiving the notice, the buyer must respond to the seller within or on a specific date, called the release date.

If the buyer fails to contact the seller within such date, it will mean that the contingency is satisfied. In such a scenario, the buyer will not be able to back out of the transaction.

3. Financial Contingency

The financial contingency is also known as "mortgage contingency." It is there to give buyers some time to apply for financing for purchasing a property. It protects the buyer as it allows them to secure funds for the purchase from a mortgage broker, bank, or any private lenders.

A financial contingency mentions a specified number of days for availing financing. At the end of such days, the buyer can terminate the contract if they can't get any funds. However, the buyer may get an extension if the seller agrees to it in writing. Otherwise, the buyer automatically becomes obligated to purchase the property regardless of whether they have secured a loan or not.

4. Sale of Another Property Contingency

In most cases, buyers can easily sell their previous property when looking to purchase a different one. However, sometimes, timing and financing don't work out in their favor. That's where home contingency steps in to protect the buyer.

A home contingency gives buyers a limited time to sell their existing home so that they can finance a new one. This contingency acts as a shield for the buyers in case they fail to sell their current property. It also works if the buyers are unable to sell the property for at least the asking price and the buyer has to back out of the deal.

This contingency can be a bit harsh on the sellers who may have to pass up another offer while waiting for the buyer's approval only to find out that the buyer backed out of the deal. But then again, this contingency is to protect the buyer. However, the seller does have the right to cancel the contract if the buyer is unable to sell their house within the specified number of days.

Top Real Estate Negotiation Tactics

Your clients may be smart and successful individuals in their own right, but most likely, they are not always good at negotiations. That's why they decide to hire you in the first place. They expect you to get them the best deal out there. This is your moment to shine and show them why hiring your services was the right choice!

What makes realtors special is our ability to close the deal that to some extent, if not entirely, is in favor of our clients. The main goal of executing our job is to have a happy client in the end and who pays us our share of the deal.

One of the main qualities of a top producer is narrowing down negotiations to the basic argument, the price. That's because it results in one winner and one loser rather than a win-win situation. You have to make sure that your client is on the winning side.

Before initiating negotiations, you must ask both buyers and sellers enough questions to learn about their primary objectives.

The criteria must include financial needs, cash requirement for closing the deal, potential relocation in the future, closing date, warranty needs for the property, number of people living in the house, physical additions to the property and many more factors.

By setting specific criteria, you can create a win-win situation for both the parties. It would be beneficial for you, especially if both the buyer and the seller are your clients. Giving them a great deal will add to your credibility.

The following are some of the strategies that you can

use to create a win-win situation:

1. Nibbling

If you are representing the buyer, then you need to get them as much amenities as possible. When someone spends a hefty amount of money on purchasing a property, they expect top-notch service. After all, they are making an investment of a lifetime. The buyer has full right to ask for certain improvements or additional work on the property. You must ensure that the seller agrees to them, especially if the buyer is willing to pay the market price for the property.

Let's understand this scenario through an example. You have a client who has agreed to pay $600,000 for a property. This client demands that some work is done on the roof or they ask for a renovation of the interior walls and flooring. It is your duty to convince the seller to agree for providing such repairs. However, make sure that the buyer is truly interested in closing the deal. They won't back out after all work has been done.

Seller's Perspective: If you are representing the seller, then your focus should be on saving your client's money and giving them a hassle-free deal.

If you are representing both parties, then you need to find a middle ground where both sides win.

2. The Hot-Potato Scenario

I do not recommend this strategy when you are representing the buyer. However, you must be aware of it. Many real estate agents do apply it out in the field.

In this strategy, buyers express the issues that are keeping them from purchasing the property in question. Instead of resolving their issues on their own, buyers tell their problems to sellers or the realtors representing the seller.

For example, the price for the property in question is $600,000. The buyer is interested in making the purchase, but they do not have sufficient cash for the down payment. Through this option, the buyer can ask for installments or other similar tactics to score the deal.

Seller's Perspective: If you are representing the seller, never allow this deal to go through. You need to stand your ground and demand full payment. The personal and financial issues of the buyer are not your concern. However, you may consider the buyer's issues if you have a long-standing relationship with them, or you trust them enough to know they won't back out on their deal.

Personal issues, financing, commissions, and delays are not the seller's problem. You must keep the seller safe in this situation and reject the offer if the situation doesn't seem to be turning into your favor.

3. The Good Guy, Bad Guy

A real estate agent can easily be compared to an advocate who represents their clients in front of the opposing party. So, if you are representing the buyer, the hero of your story is the buyer and the seller, resultantly, becomes the villain. With this strategy in mind, your ambitions are clear. You know who you have to benefit and who do you need to exploit for closing the deal in favor of your client.

For example, during negotiations, the buyer presents the seller with a huge list of requests to be completed for the deal to go through. However, the seller straightforwardly vetoes all requests. This constant refusal eventually exhausts the buyer, and they start to lose interest. It is up to you to negotiate and convince the seller to accept some if not all, requests to benefit both parties.

Seller's Perspective: Representing the seller, you need to make sure that at least some of the relevant requests are fulfilled by your client. This will keep the buyer's interest intact and close the deal on a positive note.

4. The Long Wait

This strategy is quite beneficial for the buyers but not so much for the sellers. What it does is that it takes the seller "off the table" regarding their willingness to sell. The buyer shows an interest and enters into negotiation with the seller for the purchase of the property. However, they try to hold the deal off and wait for a better offer to arrive. If you are representing the buyer, then it is a great strategy for you to create several options for your clients.

Seller's Perspective: Of course, if you are on the seller's side, then this strategy can hurt your client. The best way to avoid such offers is to create competition in the market. This will not only get your client a good price, but it will also make sure that the property is sold in time.

To do this, submit the property to an auction site and add an end date of its availability. Announce that all offers will be reviewed on a certain date and time.

Negotiating a great deal for your clients is your primary job as a realtor. If you do it right, you will be able to gain forever clients!

Chapter 8

Selling the Property

"A real estate agent has two property listings. Now add 11 more. What does the agent have now? Happiness. That agent has happiness."

- *Tim Dulany*

In the previous chapter, we discussed the shenanigans of negotiating terms for your clients. We took a general perspective of both the buyer and the seller. I mentioned some strategies and tips at the end of the chapter on how to hone your negotiation skills and execute them effectively. In this chapter, we will purely discuss how to sell a property and what skills should a top producer possess.

The first thing you need to do after receiving a call from a seller is to ask for some time to prepare a listing presentation. After preparing the presentation, make sure to arrange a meeting with the seller so you can get on the same page with them. After agreeing on the date and time to meet, go and meet them but go fully prepared. You must have all the presentation material and necessary paperwork with you, assuming you can close the deal in your first meeting.

One of the main agendas of this meeting should be to negotiate the terms of the exclusive right to the selling agreement. This is important as it binds sellers to avail only your services for selling their property. Once this agreement is signed, you can be free of worry because that contract isn't going anywhere. However, this doesn't mean that you can upset the client through delays or ridiculous offers. Instead, you should take advantage of this trust from your client and work hard to get them the best deal.

If you are a new realtor, then you need to convince the seller about your competence. No one is going to put blind trust in an agent with no prior experience in the field. Therefore, you will have to use your expertise.

After you have successfully convinced your potential client, the next you should do is establish an inventory. Having your inventory is another way to boost your credibility in front of the clients. If a realtor is only dependent on the MLS, then the clients might doubt their ability.

Marketing is a crucial part of selling a property. As a real estate top producer, you must be a marketing expert. However, this doesn't mean that your only marketing skill should be to advertise the property that you are trying to sell for your client. Anyone with a decent knowledge of the market can do that. Great realtors focus more on marketing themselves.

As a realtor, your main goal should be to be easily recognized by the people of the area that you are working in. You should be like a local celebrity. So, if someone sees your picture or name written somewhere, they will automatically believe that you are successful. People will start coming to you instead of you chasing clients around.

To become a top producer, you must always be on the course of learning about the market. Never think that you have learned enough because the market is constantly changing, and you need to stay updated.

The real estate market is a highly competitive field, and it takes a lot to stand out here. Some of the most common ways of marketing yourself are by handing out business cards to every person you meet. By every person, I mean EVERY person. It doesn't have to be a formal or official meeting. You can hand out cards in any social gathering. This is the best way to market yourself.

Another great way to get remembered by people is establishing a quote or a catchphrase. For example, you can always remind people about yourself by telling them that you are "the most reliable agent in town" or anything that clicks their mind.

When it comes to marketing of the property, the best way today is by listing it on real estate magazines, newspapers, postcards, and real estate websites such as Zillow.

Special listings require special marketing techniques, such as a custom logo or a full page ad. Realtors use these methods to get the property sold at the right price. Therefore, the main objective of a real estate agent is to get the attention of the buyers.

Once you get the interest from a buyer, you will receive a contract from their side that you need to present to your seller. The contract will feature the price that the buyer is willing to pay and other demands such as repairing or renovation of the property. As a representative of your client, you must thoroughly go through each and everything on the contract and analyze whether it is in your client's interest or not. After that, you can present the contract to your client and explain the details to them if necessary. If your client agrees with the terms on the contract, then have them sign it to close the deal. However, if your client doesn't like the contract, then they have the right to reject it altogether or counter the buyer by making some changes on the contract.

This is where you will be needed the most by your seller for negotiation (just as we discussed in the previous chapter).

After the negotiations are done and both parties agree on the latest form of contract, then both of them should sign it. The real estate agent representing the buyer will then guide them through all the necessities before making the purchase such as inspections, financing, repairs, and closing. Meanwhile, you wait for them to get all this over with. You must attend the closing of the deal with your client to make sure everything is carried out smoothly. If any problem or confusion arise, then you should take care of everything. One thing you need to keep in mind is that you will not be paid on the closing table. Instead, your commission is taken to the broker of the real estate company, and the broker will pay you after cutting the brokerage percentage.

Best Tactics of Selling the Property

Now that you are familiar with all the mechanics of the selling process, let's look at some of the best tactics of selling a property as a real estate agent:

1. Start Marketing After Signing the Listing Agreement

I have emphasized already on the importance of marketing several times throughout the book. The reason for that is obvious; it can make or break your career as a realtor. The same theory applies when we talk about selling the property for your client. Once you have got the contract and secured your position, it is time to get to work on the marketing process.

a. Harness the Social Media Power

If you have not been living under the rock for the past two decades, then you would be aware of the immensity of social media. The social media platforms today are the biggest social gatherings in the world with almost half the entire world population using it.

It is one of the best tools for real estate agents to garner clients online and also help them buy or sell properties here. Platforms such as Facebook, Twitter, Instagram, and many others can be great for attracting buyers for the listed property. All you have to do is post pictures, videos, and details of the property there and circulate it among the target audience. This is one of the best ways to get your client's property sold quickly.

b.   Keep In Touch with Your Fellow Agents

Another great way to quickly sell a property is by informing its availability to your fellow brokers. Usually, a brokerage offers an intranet for the agents so that they exclusively communicate with each other. In this way, you may be able to find a suitable buyer for your property rapidly. For example, a colleague of yours is representing a buyer who is looking for a property in the same area that your client is trying to get rid of theirs. By letting everyone in your circle know, you will be able to find the buyer pretty easily.

c.   Use the Good Old Real Estate Sign

It may be an outdated marketing method, but it still works. Installing a "For Sale" sign outside the property alerts everyone in the area who drives or walks by it. Make sure to put your contact details on the sign as well because interested buyers would want to bid in as soon as possible.

2. Stage Your Listing

One effective tactic to attract buyers is staging your listed property to make it as presentable as possible. The reason for that is because whenever a buyer sees a home online for the first time, they imagine themselves living there. Staging can enhance their imagination and develop their interest.

To stage a property, you have to adjust the decoration of the house. Make sure every furniture in the house is in the right place. You would also need to make sure only to capture the best bits of the house.

Here are some of the advantages of staging your property:

- It creates an impeccable first impression on the potential buyers and enhances their interest.
- It highlights the best features of the property and hides all its shortcomings.
- The visiting buyers also get a good first impression by getting the idea of how good they can set this house themselves.
- The presence of furniture tempts the buyers to sit down and spend some more time at the property, hence developing further interest.

3. Hire a Professional Photographer

Hiring a professional photographer should be on your agenda when trying to sell a property. However, you need to be careful during the hiring process. That's because there are some wannabe photographers out there with DSLR cameras who claim to be professional. They may be good at snapping portraits and landscapes, but they are of no use when it comes to real estate photography. What you should be looking for in their skill set is the understanding of the architecture of properties. These professionals have the best idea on how to capture the house in the best way possible. Therefore, it is better for you to look for professionals who have some experience in real estate property.

A true architectural photographer knows how to capture the best shots of the property because they have developed an image through their experience. They will move the stuff and furniture here and there until they get the perfect shot.

You can use these professional photographs on your website, social media accounts, or real estate websites for the public to see and interact.

4. Get Your Visibility As Much Views as Possible

So you have posted your listing on your social media accounts and your website, but there is no one there to see it. All your efforts would be in vain. Therefore, the next thing you want to do is advertise the listed property to get it more visible.

The very first thing you need to do is publish your listing on the MLS and all the other major real estate platforms such as Zillow, Realtor.com, and Trulia. Make sure to claim those listings so you can follow the statistics. However, there is more you can do to get more views on your listings.

i.   List It on Facebook

Facebook marketplace is gigantic. Posting your listing over there can lead to overwhelming response especially from the younger buyers.

ii.   Use Your Email Lists

The collaboration of real estate agents is quite common here in the United States. You should never underestimate the power of email list. Develop a habit to send property to your contact list that is comprised of your fellow agents and frequent buyer customers. Always keep the subject line of the email interesting and relevant to increase the open rate of your emails.

iii.   Keep Changing the Cover Photo

This is a simple trick, but it works every time. Most of the buyers use the internet to search for properties to purchase. They use platforms like Zillow, and one of the main things that they notice is the main cover photo of the listing. Therefore, it is possible that frequent searchers are simply going to ignore your listing because it would seem old and familiar to them. Periodically changing the cover photo can be quite effective to gain the interest of such people.

iv.   Host Open House Visits

Open house visits are traditional methods for attracting buyers that are still looking to make a purchase. Such events not only allow potential buyers to experience the space physically, but they also popularize your listings on all online platforms and give your property renewed attention.

v.   Broadcast on Facebook and Instagram Live

To entertain those people who cannot make it in

person, you can hold a Livestream event on Facebook or Instagram. You can give the viewers a virtual tour while answering their questions at the same time. It isn't just a video tour of the property, but the potential clients also get to interact with you and know you as a professional.

There are several other methods and tricks that you can use to sell your property as long as it works for you. The most important thing, however, is to get your clients the best deals and satisfy them in every way with your service. In this way, they are most likely to avail your services next time as well or at least refer you to others.

Chapter 9

Conclusion

"Find out where the people are going and buy the land before they get there."

- *William Penn Adair*

The first chapter of the book was merely an introduction of the book, where I discussed the 15 principles of becoming a successful realtor. The principles comprised of all the qualities that a top producer must possess.

In the second chapter, I explained in intricate details of what a top producer is and how they stand out among the regular real estate agents. I also discussed the checklist that you need to tick off before joining a brokerage which featured:

- Training
- Support
- Programs/Software
- Commission Split
- Location of the office

Later on in this chapter, I shed some light on the basic process of any realtor. This was a sixteen step process:

1. Goals
2. Knowledge of Your Farm Area
3. Knowledge of Contracts
4. Time Management

5. Prospecting
6. Leads
7. Schedule Appointments
8. Showings
9. Listings
10. Contracts
11. Closings
12. CMA
13. $$$$
14. Hire Help
15. Follow Up
16. Referrals

The third chapter is completely based on the training regime of a top producer. Here I explained the typical process of which a realtor has to go through to kick start their career.

I have dedicated the fourth chapter to marketing, which is perhaps one of the most important skills that a top producer must possess. You must be aware of all the traditional and latest marketing methods to capitalize on the market and deliver the best service for your clients.

From chapter 5 to chapter 8, I explained basic scenarios that a realtor has to face pretty much daily. Within these chapters, I also answered the questions regarding how a top producer must react in these cases.

What should you do when you receive a call from a potential customer? What should you do after you have spoken to the customer? How to negotiate the terms? How to sell a property? I have answered all of these questions in incredible length in the chapters of this book.

In the end, I would like to emphasize the importance

of one thing that all of us have, and it is very limited. I am talking about time.

Time management is the key to become a top producer in the real estate industry. Being capable of efficiently managing your time provides you the ability to do many things in a shorter period. The world of real estate demands a lot of work in a limited amount of time. You won't be able to sell millions of dollars' worth of real estate one day if you do not know how to manage your tasks promptly.

Another important characteristic of a top producer is to follow up on their customers. Following up ensures that the customers remember you whenever they need to buy or sell their property. It not only increases your credibility as a trustworthy agent, but it also serves as a brilliant customer service. You also get to develop a good relationship with your clients and even befriend some of them. They are also most likely to refer you to their social circle hence increasing your clientele and making you more money.

I would also suggest you stay in touch with your customers on a personal level. Ask them about how their life's going and tell them to remember you if they need anything. Note down all the information you can and reach out to them on important events through email or a call. I follow a rule where I send at least five emails and making five calls within a year to my customers. Lastly, I always ask them for any referral, as you should. Finally, at the end of the year, send all your customers a postcard or a Christmas card during the holiday season.

I hope this book will help develop you into a top producer in the next 12 months. I have poured all of my wisdom and experience, as well as everything I have learned in my career as a realtor in this book. If you want to be a top producer in real estate, I highly recommend to follow the tips and tricks I have jot down in this book.

Good Luck!

www.ingramcontent.com/pod-product-compliance
Lightning Source LLC
Chambersburg PA
CBHW072212170526
45158CB00002BA/571